Dogs and pets in fostering and adoption

Paul Adams

coramBAAF
ADOPTION & FOSTERING ACADEMY

Contents

Published by
CoramBAAF Adoption and Fostering Academy
41 Brunswick Square
London WC1N 1AZ
www.corambaaf.org.uk

Coram Academy Limited, registered as a company limited by guarantee in England and Wales number 9697712, part of the Coram group, charity number 312278

British Library Cataloguing in Publication Data
A catalogue record for this book is available from the British Library

ISBN 978 1 910039 25 0

Project management by Jo Francis, Publications, CoramBAAF
Designed and typeset by Helen Joubert Design
Printed in Great Britain by the Lavenham Press

Acknowledgements

A number of people have contributed to the development of this Good Practice Guide. Ian Millar's original Practice Note, *Placing Children with Dog-Owning Families* (2003), significantly influenced the content, and some material has been directly reproduced. Ian also offered helpful advice, for which I am grateful.

I am also grateful to the numerous BAAF staff who provided comments, ideas, and suggested resources: Keith Miller, Florence Merredew, Catherine Mullin, Jacqui Lawrence, Alexandra Conroy Harris, Julia Feast, Mary Bollan, Lynrose Kirby, Gareth Lambert, Non Davies, Rhona Pollock, Nicky Probert, and Catriona Walker. Thanks also to Sarah Bevan (independent social worker), Roger Chapman and Elaine Dibben for their comments on earlier drafts and to Mary Francis (social worker) for her extensive case examples.

Katrina Wilson, Fiona Letendrie and Harina Patel at BAAF all contributed to the research, and John Simmonds provided his usual wise guidance. I am also grateful to Shaila Shah and Jo Francis for their advice and editorial expertise on content and style.

Dan French and Jane Elston at BAAF, and Dominic Stevenson at Fostering Network, assisted by seeking foster carer and adopter experiences via social media, and I am grateful to them, and of course to those foster carers, adopters and social workers who shared their stories. With permission, some stories are reproduced here in full or in part, with minor style editing.

Louise Lee (Blue Cross Media Officer) pointed me in the direction of various useful documents, and Caroline Reay (Blue Cross vet) and Claire Stallard (Blue Cross animal behaviourist) helpfully corrected and improved aspects of the manuscript.

Unsurprisingly, there have been many different views and perspectives expressed, and the responsibility for any identified shortcomings in this book must ultimately rest with the author.

This book has been kindly supported by funding from the Esmeé Fairbairn Foundation.

Note about the author

Paul Adams qualified as a social worker in 1993, having been inspired by working as a foster carer in the US, and has a background in local authority children's services, managing child care and fostering teams. He is an experienced panel Chair, interim manager, consultant, trainer, and adopter.

Paul joined BAAF (now CoramBAAF) as a Fostering Development Consultant in 2010. He has authored good practice guides on parent and child fostering, contact in permanent placements, social work with Gypsy, Roma and Traveller children, and undertaking checks and references in fostering and adoption assessments. Paul has developed Form C (Connected Persons), Form FR (Fostering Reviews), both with accompanying good practice guidance, and has considerably revised Form F (Fostering Assessments) in England.

Paul lives in North Wales with his partner Sarah, and rescue dog Simba.

Chapter 1
Introduction

Since one in four families in the UK owns a dog, and nearly half of all families have a pet (PFMA, 2014), it is no surprise that questions about dogs and pets in fostering and adoption are commonplace, and this Good Practice Guide aims to provide advice for social workers, foster carers, adopters, and panel members. The main focus is on dogs, and the guide includes information about the advantages and challenges of owning dogs when fostering or adopting, matters for consideration in assessment, and advice about managing issues that might arise during placement. The guide also looks at the relevance of other pets in fostering and adoption, and provides both general principles and specific information that may be helpful.

Attitudes to dogs and pets vary considerably. For some people, dogs are "man's best friend"; significant family members bringing loyalty and friendship that have huge benefits for the health and well-being of people. It is also generally recognised that dogs can perform useful tasks for humans in traditional working roles, and increasingly in a range of therapeutic contexts. For others, however, dogs are potentially dangerous animals primarily associated with injury and disease; noisy nuisances responsible for fouling public spaces and intimidating people. Attitudes to other animals, particularly pets like rodents and reptiles, can also invoke strong feelings, both positive and negative.

People's attitudes will be influenced by various factors, including culture, belief system, and previous individual experience, and the issues arising from this can be played out in fostering and adoption contexts where dogs and other pets are involved. It is important to be mindful of this so that judgements do not unfairly characterise people as oversentimental with a "substitute child", or alternatively as hard-hearted individuals whose attitudes are incompatible with providing sensitive empathic care to children. It is also important to recognise and respect minority perspectives in relation to living with dogs or other pets.

Some politicians and high profile figures have publicly mocked social workers for an excessive interest in and caution around the issue of pets and dogs in adoption, for example, with references to a 'bloated' assessment process characterised by a 'six page dog assessment' (Gove, 2011). However, news stories report dogs biting children, often in family homes, and children have been bitten by adopters' and foster carers' dogs. Other children have experienced placement disruptions because of issues relating to animals in the home, and they might feel that a thorough consideration of this aspect of the family is time well spent. The contributions from adopters, foster carers and social workers throughout this practice guide should serve to illustrate this point.

This practice guide has been developed alongside an assessment form for dogs (Appendix A) and an assessment form for other pets (Appendix B). Completed examples of these forms are included in this book as Appendices C and D. Sample forms are also available in the members' section of the CoramBAAF website (www.corambaaf.org.uk). The forms are provided free to all licence holders of CoramBAAF's fostering and adoption assessment forms.

This guide is also intended to be helpful in assisting fostering services and adoption agencies to develop carefully considered, logical and proportionate policies in relation to dogs and other pets. Although the guide is written specifically in relation to fostering and adoption, it will apply equally to other legal arrangements such as special guardianship.

Chapter 2
Information about dogs

DOGS AND THE LAW

For the most part, the law around dog ownership in England and Wales is relatively straightforward. Under the Control of Dogs Order 1992, there is a requirement that in public places dogs wear a collar that provides details of the owner's name and address, but Government announcements suggest that microchipping will become a legal requirement in Wales in 2015 and in England in 2016. Under the Dangerous Dogs Act 1991 (as amended in 1997 and 2014), it is an offence if a dog is 'dangerously out of control', and there was a requirement for certain breeds or types of dog that are defined as dangerous to have been registered within a certain time period, which has now elapsed.

The Animal Welfare Act 2006 sets out offences around causing or allowing a dog to suffer unnecessarily, or failing to meet the dog's basic needs. Fouling is covered under the Clean Neighbourhoods and Environment Act 2005, and noise nuisance is addressed in the Environmental Protection Act 1990. Other specific matters are addressed by the Breeding of Dogs Act 1973 (as amended by the Sale of Dogs Act 1999) and the Animal Boarding Establishments Act 1963, both of which set out requirements about being licensed with the local authority.

Very similar legislation applies in Scotland and Northern Ireland where the breed-specific elements of the Dangerous Dogs Act 1991 also apply. In Scotland, other matters are set out in the Control of Dogs (Scotland) Act 2010 and the Animal Health and Welfare (Scotland) Act 2006; the most notable difference from England and Wales is the provision for dog control notices, known informally as "dog Asbos". In Northern Ireland, the key legislation is the Dogs (Northern Ireland) Order 1983 and the Welfare of Animals Act (Northern Ireland) 2011, and Northern Ireland differs from other UK countries in requiring that dogs are both licensed and microchipped.

BREEDS

The Kennel Club recognises 196 breeds of dog, broadly classified in line with their original function, and under two main headings: sporting and non-sporting. Sporting dogs are further classified into terriers, gundogs and hounds. Non-sporting dogs are divided in the pastoral group, the working group, the utility group, and the toy group. The Kennel Club publishes "breed standards", describing temperament and characteristics of different breeds, which can be accessed at the Kennel Club's Breed Information Centre on their website (see Useful Organisations).

In terms of fostering and adoption, the breed of the dog is important in that certain breeds have evolved for guarding and protection, or for herding or tackling other animals, and these may pose more of a potential risk to children than breeds that have evolved primarily as companions to people. Put simply, some breeds will be potentially more dangerous than others, either due to physical attributes such as size and jaw structure, or as the result of temperament, or both. It is suggested that when undertaking a dog assessment, the breed of the dog is checked using the Kennel Club website.

However, it is important to understand that breed is only relevant up to a point: dogs are "individuals", and their behaviour will be determined by a number of factors including their history and the way that they are trained and managed. Although the Kennel Club does ascribe characteristics wholesale to particular breeds, this should be seen as a general guide only. It is misguided, and even dangerous, to assume that all dogs in one particular breed are either savage and unpredictable, or friendly and trustworthy, and each dog should be considered as an individual in its own right.

Contrary to the principle of considering each dog as an individual, the Dangerous Dogs Act 1991 (as amended in 1997 and 2014) called for the registration of certain dogs 'belonging to types bred for fighting' and lists the Japanese Tosa, Dogo Argentino, Fila Braziliero, and the Pit Bull Terrier (which is not actually recognised as a breed by the Kennel Club). While it is widely acknowledged that the Dangerous Dogs Act is fundamentally flawed, in that it identifies dangerous breeds or types of dog and ignores how they are brought up, trained and owned (see Dogs Trust, undated e; Kennel Club, 2009), it is understandable that fostering services and adoption agencies have tended to consider that dog breeds named under this legislation are incompatible with fostering or adoption.

Dangerous Dogs Act

According to the Kennel Club (2009), 'it is generally accepted that the Dangerous Dogs Act 1991 is the most discredited piece of legislation on the statute book'. Notwithstanding the subsequent amendments, the Dangerous Dogs Act Study Group – an umbrella group representing a number of organisations including the Kennel Club, Dogs Trust, Blue Cross, British Veterinary Association and Royal College of Veterinary Surgeons – continues to press for legislation that is based entirely on how the dog *behaves* rather than on what it looks like.

There are other breeds or types that for reason of size or role have been identified as more potentially dangerous than others. While there might be some justification in identifying the potential dangers from these breeds, it is just that – a potential. Membership of a breed says nothing about the individual dog in question, and to make judgements on this basis is not scientifically meaningful or logically justifiable. However, in practice some fostering services have determined that certain breeds of dog are incompatible with fostering younger children – an unhelpfully rigid approach.

Poor practice example

One local authority fostering service policy states that:

Only children over 11 will be placed with families who have the following dogs:

- *Alsatian (German Shepherd)*
- *Rottweiler*
- *Doberman*
- *Bull Terrier (Staffordshire)*
- *Bulldog*
- *Rhodesian Ridgeback*
- *Border Collie*

Only children over 11 will be placed with families who own two or more dogs of any breed.

This policy, although recognising some managerial scope for divergence, is unhelpful in that it targets particular breeds without evidence to justify this, and risks preventing very suitable families from fostering younger children, simply because they own a particular breed of dog, or own two dogs. It ignores the fact that this dog or dogs might be impeccably behaved, have lived with young children for many years, or may even have separate living space from the human family members.

Many dogs are "cross-breeds" or "mongrels" meaning that they have ancestry from two or more different recognised breeds. It should be noted that the Kennel Club does not recognise cross-breeds, and so in checking their website it would be necessary to look at the known ancestry of the dog in terms of the recognised breeds. For example, a labradoodle will need to be considered in terms of both labrador and poodle characteristics.

Chapter 3
Advantages and disadvantages of keeping dogs as pets

THE ADVANTAGES OF DOGS

Emotional well-being

Dogs provide a real source of companionship and unconditional affection for both adults and children. Many children joining new families may be anxious or afraid to make overtures to the humans in the household, and the dog might be able to provide a more available listening ear (see Rockett, 2014). Where children's rejecting behaviour can drive humans to respond with hurt and anger, dogs are less likely to get caught up in these relatively subtle dynamics. A literature review of scientific and academic publications (Dogs Trust, 2011) provides clear evidence to show that dog ownership is inversely related to loneliness, isolation and depression in humans.

Although not specific to fostering and adoption, there are a number of studies that highlight the therapeutic benefits of dogs in different settings. Some identify the benefits that dogs bring for autistic children (Burgoyne et al, 2014), and in greater socialisation for disabled children. In certain contexts, such as during hospital examinations, the mere presence of a dog has been found to reduce levels of stress and anxiety in children (Dogs Trust, 2011), and one study that looked at group therapy for children who had been sexually abused (Dietz et al, 2012, p 665) concluded that 'children in the groups that included therapy dogs showed significant decreases in trauma symptoms including anxiety, depression, anger, post-traumatic stress disorder, dissociation, and sexual concerns'.

Fostered children in Rockett's (2014) study reported that animals (mainly dogs) in the foster home made them feel calmer and less stressed. There is also evidence to suggest that, for people who are not experiencing particular stresses, there are still 'many positive psychological and physical benefits for [pet] owners' (McConnell et al, 2011, p 1239).

Barbara (foster carer)

We have had a dog all the time we have been fostering, and over the years I have noticed how children can often talk through the dog to me, and seen how they have all enjoyed loving and walking the dog. Our current placement is a disabled child with complex health needs, and his life was very fragile. We were told that he was possibly blind, but I noticed that he could see the dog. I believe the child has learnt to move because he wants to get to the dog; now he rolls all over the floor after the dog, even though the child has neurological brain damage, and by all accounts should not be able to move like this. He can even sign "dog".

Gilligan (2009, p 70) spells out the emotional benefits of animals more generally and in relation to children in care:

> *An animal may be warm, cuddly, responsive, loyal, non-judgemental, sensitive, reliable and constant. It can contain the secrets and stresses confided within it. This "listening ear" which an animal may provide may be very therapeutic for a child who finds it hard to access what he or she regards as a trustworthy human ear ... The animal can represent a comforting, precious and supportive constancy. It may signal very clearly its affection for the child, a child who may have been starved of such affection at many points in the past. The purring of a cat, the nuzzling by a horse, the wagging tail of a dog directed in recognition of a child familiar to the animal may prove healing gifts for the child craving acceptance and affection. This sense of "lovability" conveyed to the child by the animal may help to improve self-esteem.*

Attachment

Rockett (2014) and Rockett and Carr (2014) go further than this, and evidence how dogs serve the function of attachment figures in line with the understanding of attachment theory and the secure base model. Rockett offers specific examples from a study of the lived experience of children in long-term foster care to show how this applies in relation to providing a safe haven, a secure base from which to explore the world, and in relation to separation distress and proximity maintenance. It is noted from the wider literature that humans are more likely to form attachment relationships with animals when they have fewer social networks, and this will often apply to children in foster care or adoption.

In addition to a pet serving as an attachment figure, Rockett (2014, p 230) suggests that 'an animal's presence within the foster environment may facilitate human–human relationships from an attachment perspective'. This happens in two ways. The first is through "softening" – how the animal influences the child's perception of the foster home. This can include the dog serving as a "transitional object" for the child, offering an opportunity for safe, shared experiences with the carer, and through recognising that if the carer is kind and loving to the dog, then they may well demonstrate the same approach to the child. The second aspect is "switching", which relates to how the child originally develops trust in the animal, and later, having recognised the trust between animal and carer, develops that trust and attachment directly.

Fostered children speaking

I like spending time with Socks and I used to hide in [the living room] with him when there was a knock at the door. I used to worry it was the social worker coming to take me away. I didn't feel safe without Socks and when I was with him, holding his ears, I felt relaxed and I wouldn't have the big thumping in my body.

I heard Rose talking to Socks about things about me. I heard her telling him to be nice to me and not to feel jealous because she still loved him. She said that I seemed really nice and that she wanted to get to know me. I sat on the stairs and listened and watched her through the rails. It made me feel funny in my tummy when she said those nice things, and when I saw that she was talking to Socks I liked it so I started talking to him too.

(Rockett, 2014)

Fostered children speaking

I find it easier to talk about difficult stuff with Gilly or Rich when Scruff is around. He doesn't really do anything special, but just knowing he is there makes it easier to do things that are tough.

When bad stuff happens, or I have a really bad day, Scruff's very slow and quiet. He looks at me different, like he knows something is up, but he doesn't quite know what. But he's always trying … he's there the whole time. And he, like, seems to act the same way I feel – like he knows what I'm really feeling. Weird in a way 'cos it's like he can read my thoughts. Sometimes … when things are really bad, I like being with him because I like having a cuddle and he never seems to really get stressed. I like that. He seems calm the whole time, and always there.

Sometimes I don't get stuff from Gilly or Rich when I need it, and that's when Scruff is around for me. And that's when I like it. I don't have to feel bad about saying things to him. He doesn't tell people – because he can't!

(Rockett, 2014)

Health and physical well-being

A summary and review of research (Dogs Trust, 2011) also correlates dog ownership with good physical health in terms of both adults and children having increased exercise, and reduced likelihood of being overweight or obese, although this only applies where dog owners actually walk their dogs. In some studies, dog ownership has been linked with reduced diabetes risk and reduced blood pressure. While this might link with the increased exercise, in some experiments it is the physical touch – stroking the dog – that is associated with beneficial outcomes. A number of studies have also suggested that, where children were brought up in dog-owning families, they had a reduced risk of developing allergies, asthma and eczema (Dogs Trust, 2011).

Resilience and leisure interest

Dogs can provide a great source of fun and interest, and children can derive great satisfaction from attending dog clubs and dog shows, participating in dog training or obedience and agility competitions, or from simply teaching their dog to "do tricks" in the garden. Even just walking the dog allows the child to experience the pleasures of the outdoors, to have space for reflection and talking, and to meet with other dog-walkers. It can also provide a focus for conversation that gives children something in common with peers, or can offer a well-rehearsed "script" that can be used in conversations with new adults, allowing for the practice and development of social skills. In some situations, early experiences with dogs in the home can be the start of an interest that leads to employment or a career in later life.

Where children are offered an opportunity to share in the care and responsibility for the dog, this will likely assist in their sense of achieving competence, being trusted with something important, and experiencing a sense of what it feels like to take care of another living being. Through the dog, children can learn about meeting the needs of others, using power appropriately, and protecting the vulnerable with care and consideration. This can help with their self-image and can play an important part in developing resilience (see Gilligan, 2009).

Sense of family membership

Dogs are often seen as full and integrated members of the family, and it can be helpful for fostered or adopted children to find a position within the family that involves relationships with both human and canine members. Where they have a responsibility for sharing in the dog's care or routines, this can help to cement a sense of their place in the family. More generally, the dog can provide a focus for shared family events: going for a walk together, visiting the vet, or simply playing in the garden. Where dogs have been acquired from rescue centres, this can sometimes provide a unique and safe opportunity for children to think about and discuss their own experiences of being ill-treated or neglected in their birth families, and to help them understand that others can provide appropriate safe care. Rockett (2014) links this to the development of attachment, and provides evidence to show that foster children would often draw parallels between their own experiences and that of dogs in the family.

Katy (adopter)

I am a single adopter and at the time of adoption I had a medium-sized mongrel dog called Toby who had come from a rescue charity about 12 years previously. Right from the beginning, Kimmy claimed Toby as "her" dog and there was an immediate bond. Kimmy enjoyed looking after Toby; she loved feeding him, making sure he had enough water, and this was really positive and facilitated conversations about how to look after animals (and children) and keep them fed and safe. Kimmy had many problems at the beginning and her life wasn't easy, but she found great comfort in our dog. Toby looked after Kimmy, followed her around, and there were many occasions when the thing that snapped her out of a full-blown tantrum was the dog. The first thing in coming out of a tantrum, she would lay on the floor cuddling him.

Kimmy came to know that I "adopted" Toby from a charity and that just like her he came from a difficult background where his first family did not look after him and hurt him. She really identified with this, and over the years I often found her talking to the dog about her feelings and emotions in a way that she found difficult to do with anyone else. I have gained a lot of insight into Kimmy's behaviours and emotions by sitting at the bottom of the stairs listening to her talk to the dog.

As Toby became older, I knew he was in pain. Telling Kimmy that we would need to have Toby "put down" was very difficult and she was distraught. I had always anticipated that this would be really difficult for Kimmy and it was. I prepared for the event quite carefully, and we made time for family photographs with Toby and had a "special day" for him when he was allowed to have any food he wanted and go to his favourite place. On the day that he was to be put to sleep, Kimmy got to say goodbye to Toby at home.

It was really difficult because I was also devastated, and it was vary hard to support both my own emotions as well as hers, but in hindsight I think this was positive in many ways because we were able to work through these really strong emotions together. Seeing me express strong emotions of sadness almost gave Kimmy "permission" to express the way she felt. Kimmy dealt with her emotions over Toby's death by looking out every photograph of him that she could find. Every night for a long time she talked about Toby before going to sleep; not easy for me, but I thought it was really positive that Kimmy found ways of dealing with the loss that worked for her.

A while later we decided to get a new puppy and this has also been a fantastic learning experience for Kimmy. She has been centrally involved in this – she was part of choosing and naming the new puppy and is involved in all aspects of her care. I have photographs of Kimmy at the vet with the new pup, wearing a stethoscope and listening to her heartbeat. She spent months looking up YouTube dog-training videos and has been responsible for teaching Molly many fun tricks as well as being part of the more serious training. Kimmy has difficulty with concentration and application to learning in school, but when the subject of learning is dog- or animal-related, she finds motivation. She is a fount of knowledge about looking after and training dogs. Having family dogs in her life has taught Kimmy about way more than having a dog.

THE DISADVANTAGES OF DOGS

Safety issues

Children do get bitten by dogs and this risk should never be minimised. There have been occurrences where children have been seriously injured or even killed by dogs, although death is very rare. Data from the NHS Health and Social Care Information Centre (2012) showed that, in 2011–12, there were nearly 6,500 hospital admissions in England as the result of injuries sustained from dog bites, with children under the age of 10 accounting for around one in every six of these admissions. Data on the types of injuries sustained showed that children had a higher rate of admission for oral and facial surgery than adults.

This means that there were just over 1,000 dog-inflicted injuries to children under the age of 10, which compares with 35,000 incidents of children under four falling down the stairs, and 50,000 children under 14 being admitted to Accident and Emergency because of burns or scalds (Child Alert, 2014). This should help to put the risk into proportion, but whatever the statistics say, for each child who is bitten by a dog, this will be a significant incident, with potential physical and psychological consequences. Adopters and foster carers need to be mindful of the risks, and take appropriate measures to manage and reduce them, as suggested elsewhere in this guide.

With larger dogs, there is also the risk of injuries from dogs jumping up or inadvertently knocking over a child. These are real risks that need to be considered carefully in the dog assessment and also at the time of matching, but in a way that is proportionate and considers both the likelihood of this happening, and the probable consequences if it does. It is normal for children to get bumps and bruises in the course of their childhood, and in most cases this does no lasting harm.

Kerry Taylor (Blue Cross Education Officer)

Most dog owners have lovely family dogs that they consider wouldn't hurt a fly. But for all dogs there are times when they can react in an unwanted way, for example, around food, when woken, in pain or stressed. There are many benefits to having a dog in the family, but it is important to know how to all live safely and happily together. Understanding your dog's body language and teaching your child how to behave around dogs are so important for both your child's safety and your dog's well-being.

(Blue Cross, 'Pet charity reveals how to help protect children around dogs', Press Release, 28 July 2014)

Mary (social worker)

Not all dogs are compatible with fostering or adoption, and not all dog owners are suitable to foster or adopt. I recall turning down a family that kept large German Shepherds as guard dogs, penned in their kitchen, barking incessantly and aggressively. The couple found it difficult to appreciate that both dogs and children can be unpredictable and even I was perturbed by the dogs' behaviour. Another family had three medium-sized terrier dogs in a small, two-bedroomed terraced house. With the dogs continuously yapping and snapping at my ankles, it was clear that space was an issue. The couple were advised to consider reducing the number of dogs but decided to prioritise their animals above their desire to adopt.

One couple with two large rescue dogs were very co-operative when I suggested that their animals might benefit from training. One dog in particular was very anxious and continuously alert for strangers walking by, or coming into the home. I assessed that there was a potential risk of the dogs becoming jealous of a child joining the family, but fortunately the couple sought help from a respected dog trainer. She taught the couple how to help the dogs to modify their behaviour around adults and children. Two young boys were subsequently placed separately in this family; both developed positive relationships with the dogs, and loved going on walks with them and their adoptive parents.

Another couple had an Old English Sheepdog. Although the assessment gave no indication of any problems, as always I mentioned that dogs can sometimes be unpredictable in their behaviour. When the couple were matched with a two-and-a-half-year-old child, we planned the introductions and the couple decided it was best if the dog was introduced to their child in a local park where it would be less inclined to be territorial. On the day in question, the child enjoyed running around in the park with the dog, until the dog jumped up and bit her just below the eye. This came as a great surprise to the adopters who took the difficult decision to immediately rehome the dog with another family member.

Robbie (social worker)

One of the families I assessed had two Staffordshire bull terriers that seemed lovely dogs. Although they barked every time I arrived for a visit, the adopters kept them in the kitchen for a while until they calmed down and that seemed to work. I saw them with children and adults during the assessment and I never saw any concerning behaviours. Also, the adopters had involved a dog psychologist who provided a report reassuring me that the dogs had lovely temperaments and did not represent a risk. We placed an 18-month-old girl with them, and the adopters proved to be fabulous parents to her.

However, a few months after the adoption order, I had to visit the family to discuss something new. When I arrived, the dogs (who were kept in the kitchen behind a stair gate) started barking, fighting each other, and being aggressive, until one of them bit the other quite badly. The male adopter went in the kitchen to separate the dogs, and one of the dogs bit his hand and broke it.

The adopters were horrified and very shaken by what had happened. They explained that, since their little girl had moved in with them, one of the dogs seemed to fight the other each time anyone arrived at the house, but this time it had gone too far. I did not even need to ask what they were going to do about it; they immediately made the decision that the aggressive dog could no longer live in the family home. But what could have happened had the two-year-old child got in between the dogs at the wrong time ...

Health risks

Dogs can carry certain zoonotic diseases (animal diseases that can be communicated to humans). It is recognised that 'younger children are at highest risk of catching these diseases due to weaker immune systems and their investigative behaviour' (Westgarth, 2010, p 10). This will also be the case for children with certain health conditions, or where behaviour is more typical of a younger child.

One specific infection is toxocariasis (NHS, 2013b), which is caused by roundworm parasites most commonly found in cats, dogs and foxes and which spreads from animals to humans via infected faeces. Puppies and kittens are more likely to be infected by toxocara than mature dogs and cats. Toxocariasis is very rare in the UK, with the Health Protection Agency suggesting an average of three reported cases each year for the decade 2000–2010 (NHS, 2013b). In most cases, people have mild symptoms such as coughs, a high temperature and headaches, but in rare cases the infection can cause severe symptoms, such as fatigue, loss of appetite, breathing difficulties, and blurred or cloudy vision. Most cases make a full recovery and do not experience any long-term complications, but there is a risk of permanent vision loss if one of the eyes is affected.

The NHS (2012) offers general pet hygiene tips to reduce the risk of infection.

- Wash your hands thoroughly. Always use an antibacterial soap after handling your pets (this is essential before preparing food).

- Teach children to always wash their hands. You could wipe their hands with a cleaning wipe, especially before they eat anything.

- Make sure children stay away from dog and cat faeces. Don't let children play around a litter tray and stay clear of dog litter bins at the park.

In relation to toxocariasis (NHS, 2013c), it is suggested that children should also wash their hands with soap and water after coming into contact with soil or sand, and should be taught about the dangers of eating these. Pets should be kept away from children's sandpits, and these should be covered when not in use. They additionally note that owners should check that their dogs (and cats) are kept clean, regularly dewormed and that faeces are properly disposed of. The NHS (2012) advises that animals should not be allowed to sleep on or in people's beds, and since dogs use their tongues for cleaning themselves, they could pass on germs by licking humans, especially around the mouth.

Cohen (2012) makes similar points about hygiene in relation to a range of pet animals, including dogs, but attempts to put the concerns into context:

> While there may seem to be a frightening list of potentially dangerous pet diseases, remember that as long as you keep your pet regularly wormed and treated for external parasites, such as ticks and fleas – and

as long as you take common sense precautions like always washing your hands thoroughly after handling animals (and before handling food!) – then the incidence of infection from pets is relatively rare. And even once infected, in many cases, the illness can be easily treated or will resolve by itself, often with no outward symptoms! It is only in rare cases that the disease will develop severe complications.

The fact is that most reasonable parents will permit children to touch animals at petting farms and the like, and they will likely do so on school trips and other outings. They will also be allowed to undertake gardening and outside play involving contact with soil and sand. For most people this is accepted as low risk, and one which is outweighed by the associated benefits. As a general rule, risk needs to be managed, not avoided, and statutory guidance in fostering reminds us that while foster carers should 'avoid unnecessary risks, excessive caution is unhelpful' (Department for Education, 2011, p 24).

Allergies and phobias

Some children are allergic to dogs (NHS, 2012), and in such cases even the most rigorous cleaning regime may not prevent allergic reactions, although it should be noted that some dogs constitute a lesser allergy risk than others (see Dogs Trust, undated b). In other situations, a child might be so afraid of dogs that living with a dog would be impossible. Both of these potential difficulties can be addressed by good matching processes, but it is essential that this is actively considered by both the placing authority and the foster carers or adopters themselves.

For foster carers in particular, they will also need to be sensitive to the fact that some of the professionals involved in a child's case might be allergic to their dog or other pet, or phobic about them, and so the carer must be willing to try and make adjustments around this as necessary. Sometimes this might be as simple as putting a dog into another room for the duration of a visit, but if things are more complicated, this might require flexibility and sensitivity from all parties.

Rachel and Caroline (adopters)

Just over a year ago, our two sons were placed with us, aged two and three years old respectively. They came from a background of severe neglect, domestic abuse and parental drug use, and their birth parents' home was often visited by drug dealers with their large dogs, demanding money. As a result, both boys came to us with an almost debilitating fear of animals. The eldest would literally freeze in fear then have a complete meltdown if he even saw a dog in his line of vision, regardless of how near or far that dog was. The youngest, seeing the absolute fear of animals in his older brother, seemed to have acquired a very similar response.

We have two cats which, unbeknown to anyone at the time of matching, induced the same response in the boys, and the first few weeks were really difficult. However, slowly but surely we worked with the boys to try and reduce the fear by taking little steps. With a lot of hand-holding and physically and emotionally containing the boys, we slowly enabled them to stand in the same room as the cats, then closer to them, then with the boys in our arms we stroked the cats until, remarkably, one day, the youngest reached out his hand and stroked our tortoiseshell himself. He was so proud and really enjoyed the softness. It took a few more weeks for our eldest to do the same but he did, and again he was so proud.

We also began to notice that, as we walked through parks, dogs would walk past us and neither boy seemed to mind. Then one incredible day, we were on a beach next to a man and a small dog. One of the boys stopped to look and the man asked them if they'd like to stroke his dog. We were about to explain that they were afraid, when both boys nodded, grasped our hands and stepped forward. They stroked a dog. They actually stroked a dog! We couldn't believe it and even now, writing this, the lump returns to my throat.

Now, a year later, both boys adore our cats, actively seeking them out, and, in fact, they seem to be a source of calmness and even therapy for our eldest. He recently announced he wanted a dog for his birthday next year!

Cultural considerations

There will be some children from particular religious or cultural groups where placement with a dog-owning family will not be appropriate. Maybe the most common example relates to Islam. In a book written specifically for foster carers of Muslim children (Khanom, 2012, p 31), it is suggested that:

> There is no prohibition on Muslims keeping pets, with the exception of dogs and pigs. Guide dogs, guard dogs and hunting dogs are acceptable however for the specific purpose that they are needed ... Please note, however, that dogs are not to be allowed to enter a place of prayer, whether that is in the young person's bedroom or in the mosque ... Many Muslim children are afraid of dogs due to lack of exposure to them.

It is important, however, not to make assumptions since not all Muslims will accept this interpretation of their religion, and some Muslim families do keep dogs as pets. It will therefore be important to listen to individual children and their families' wishes and feelings regarding this matter. Children from other minority groups may also have been brought up with, and hold particular attitudes to, dogs, that need to be carefully considered.

The risk to the dog

In some situations, children may pose a serious risk to dogs and according to the NSPCC (undated), 'animal abuse by children is quite widespread' in the UK. This aggression might be the result of their own experience of violence and abuse, or because they are impulsive or thoughtless, or simply unable to interact calmly and appropriately with the dog. If a child teases or hurts a dog, then retaliation might be the normal response, with potentially dire consequences for both the child and dog. Any information on a child's previous behaviour with animals must be considered carefully as part of the matching process.

Penny (foster carer)

As an experienced foster carer for over 25 years, I have found, sadly, that a number of children and young people will take advantage of pets' good natures if they are allowed to. I have two personal experiences of this.

The first was where an 11-year-old girl came to us in an emergency because her mother had been detained for certain offences and had not anticipated or planned for this. The girl brought with her an eight-month-old black mongrel dog. Within two days this unhappy little girl had started to take her anger out on the little dog. She was taking it for a walk to the end of the garden when I observed her from the kitchen window holding it by the throat and shaking it. I went straight out and told her gently that this was not how we treated our pets; suffice to say she was not allowed unsupervised time with the dog, and it was moved to another member of her family.

The second example was when I cared for a teenager who wanted a goldfish. Despite voicing my concern to the social worker about this plan, citing the young person's inability to care for herself, low self-esteem, and self-harming behaviour, I was overruled. Consequently the teenager squeezed the goldfish to death in a fit of anger, which was very unpleasant.

I would like to say to any carers who believe their pets are safe from children placed with them to be very aware of the potential mistreatment of their beloved furry family member. Children, especially those who have experienced domestic abuse, will often have experienced pets being treated cruelly. However, we do and always have had a dog, and now also have six chickens, and when children are well supervised it can be a very productive way for them to learn to care.

Chapter 4
Advice for dog owners

CANINE CHARACTERISTICS

Historically, dog behaviour has been interpreted in terms of pack behaviour and hierarchy, underpinned by a belief that dogs were motivated to achieve a higher status relative to other dogs and people. It was felt that in order to manage dogs effectively the human owner needed to dominate them, replicating the role of the pack leader:

In the wild, the wolf, the domestic dog's ancestor, lives in packs composed of extended family groups ... The pack is structured in a clear order or hierarchy, with a dominant male and female pair at the top of the group and other members ranked lower down, depending on age, sex and abilities. Communication is vital for the survival of the pack ... It reinforces the pecking order so that each pack member knows its place in the scheme of things.

(Stilwell, 2005, p 18)

When you are pack leader, the dog will take his cues from you and settle more confidently into your home. Some breeds of dog are naturally more dominant than others, as are some individual dogs. But all dogs are much happier and better behaved when they recognise their human owners as their pack leaders. They're happier because they are free of the stress of being in charge. They're better behaved because they know that they have to submit to your wishes to get the things that they want.

(Stilwell, 2005, p 20)

However, all of the main UK animal welfare, training and veterinary organisations (Welfare in Dog Training, 2010) reject this "pack/hierarchy/dominance model" as fundamentally flawed, arguing that it is based on a mistaken interpretation of wolf behaviour, and on a series of false assumptions about how this might apply to dogs living alongside humans. They argue that this is an outdated and unscientific approach that ignores more recent research and clinical practice that better explains the motivation and experience of dogs in domestic settings. Instead, experts now talk in terms of an attachment figure who provides a sense of safety and a secure emotional base from which the dog can explore the world:

19

Rather than trying to dominate a dog, we think it is much better to be a friend to him, train him kindly, interact with him, care for and accept him for the dog that he should be. Whilst it can be a good idea to introduce consistent common sense rules around the home that you want your dog to comply with for safety and perhaps convenience, these should be trained using positive reinforcement and not be based on trying to reduce his "dominance status". There's nothing wrong with providing some level of leadership to a dog, but remember that good leaders earn respect and trust through benevolence (kindness and generosity), not force.

(Dogs Trust, 2010)

It is important to recognise that for humans and dogs to live safely together, the human must be able to influence and manage the behaviour of the dog. It is equally important that in managing the dog, the owner does this in a way that makes the dog feel safe and secure, rather than anxious, confused or under threat. Attempts to dominate the dog through aggressive leadership may be counterproductive, and can actually make the dog more likely to respond with aggression. This is particularly the case where efforts to reinforce dominance are experienced by the dog as a punishment, or where they induce pain or fear.

I inked to this, historically there was an emphasis on "pack behaviour" being potentially problematic when more than two dogs lived together, and there has been a common misconception that "three dogs make a pack". It is now generally accepted that it is not the number of dogs that matters, but the specific behaviour of the dogs, whatever the number, and the associated behaviour of the humans in the household.

CARING FOR DOGS

While it is perfectly possible to be a safe and responsible dog owner without having any particular expertise in dog behaviour, owners do, however, need to understand some basic rules, and to understand that dogs are not humans, and experience things in a different way to people. There is much widely accepted guidance for dog owners that will help dogs feel content, and will minimise the risk of difficulties (see also References and Useful Organisations):

- Dogs need owners who are consistent and predictable and meet their needs in a way that promotes feelings of safety, security and contentment.

- All dogs need exercise and stimulation. The extent of this will depend on breed and size, but if dogs are not appropriately occupied and exercised on a daily basis, then they will become bored and undesirable behaviour will be more likely.

- Training of any sort is good for dogs in that it stimulates their minds and provides physical exercise. Owners should never train their family pet dogs to guard as this potentially increases the likelihood of aggression.

- Dog owners should carefully consider the benefits of routine annual inoculations and the use of regular treatments for worms and fleas. This is especially important if they are caring for babies or young children.

- The decision about whether or not to neuter a dog is complex (see text box), but responsible owners should think carefully about this, and take advice from a vet or other professional as appropriate.

- There may be benefits for dog owners in taking out third party liability insurance on their dogs. Sometimes cover is provided through standard household insurance, or is available at relatively low cost through membership of a dog owners' organisation or through a specific insurance policy.

Neutering

Neutering – the surgical removal of the reproductive organs in male and female dogs – is a procedure that is broadly supported by a number of organisations in relation to numbers of unwanted dogs (and cats). For male dogs this means castration (removal of the testicles), and in female dogs spaying (removal of the ovaries and uterus). Most organisations tend to emphasise the potential benefits of neutering in terms of both the health and behaviour of the dog.

However, the issues are not entirely straightforward. While in some circumstances neutering can assist with hormone-related behavioural problems in both male and female dogs, in other circumstances it can actually make things worse (Association of Pet Behaviour Counsellors, 2013a; 2013b). The Association of Pet Behaviour Counsellors (APBC) suggests that, on balance, the health benefits of neutering for female dogs outweighs the risks, but for male dogs the health risks might outweigh the benefits. They suggest that each situation should be considered on its merits.

In considering the various advice available, it is important that the assessor recognises that, while the majority of it will be broadly accepted and followed by most competent dog owners, not everyone is a perfect dog owner. Just because someone is not adhering to all of these elements does not mean that they are not suitable to adopt or foster. The assessor needs to be flexible and sensible, and consider matters in relation to a number of factors, including the size and breed of dog, and the age of the child or children under consideration. The foster carer or adopter should be considered in relation to the range of advice above, and excessive emphasis should not be placed on each single item except where this poses a real risk to any children being placed.

DOGS AND CHILDREN

Dogs will also need to interact appropriately with children. It is for the adults in the home to set the expectations, manage the interaction between dogs and children, and encourage children to behave appropriately with dogs. Stilwell (2005, p 79) suggests some very clear rules to teach children:

- *Do not tease a dog with food or toys.*

- *Do not touch a dog while he is eating.*

- *Do not touch a dog while he is sleeping. You might startle or scare him and he could react without thinking and snap at you.*

- *Never stare at a dog and never put your face close to a dog's face.*

- *Remember that your dog is an animal and not a cuddly toy. Some dogs don't like being hugged.*

- *Be gentle with your dog. Don't play rough with him.*

A number of reputable organisations confirm this advice (Dogs Trust, undated a; APBS, 2012; RSPCA, 2012; Blue Cross 2013a, 2014) and provide further guidance for adults in relation to keeping children safe around dogs:

- Socialise dogs properly with children and teach them how to behave, including not to jump up or be too boisterous as this can lead to accidents.

- Teach children to interact appropriately with dogs, including never to disturb a dog that is sleeping, eating, ill or injured, as dogs may react badly in these situations.

- Never leave young children unsupervised with any dog, even if it is only for a few minutes.

- Have separate and distinct toys for the children and for the dog.

- Provide a quiet and safe place for the dog so that they can get away from children's attention if they want to.

- Be aware of the dog's body language so that you can identify and intervene at the earliest sign of stress.

Blue Cross blog

How to stay safe around dogs: signs to look out for

Blue Cross uses a traffic light system as a means of trying to remember what a dog might be trying to say.

RED – these are dogs telling us to stop, don't come any closer and go away!

- I am afraid. I am crouching and may crawl away. My ears are flat back to my head and I am growling.

- I am bold and stand my ground. The hairs on the back of my neck stand up and my body is tense.

- When I feel vulnerable I will move away from you then roll over. Lots of people get this sign mixed up and want to chase after me and try to tickle my belly. Remember, if I move away, I don't want you to be close!

YELLOW – these are dogs telling us I'm not sure about you yet, please keep away.

- I move slowly and lower my head. I raise a paw and lick my lips to show I am uncertain.

- I am moving away from you with my head lowered, tail tucked between my legs and possibly glancing sideways, showing the white of my eyes.

- My head is down with my tail between my legs. I might yawn to show you I am still not sure about you.

GREEN – these are dogs telling us they are a little happier to see us!

- My body is relaxed, my ears are forward and my tail and body are wagging.

- I want to play! This is my play bow; front legs straight forward, bottom raised and tail wagging.

- My face is interested and alert; I have a relaxed jaw and a hanging tongue.

https://www.bluecross.org.uk/pet-advice/be-safe-dogs

Note: the original source better illustrates these signs to look out for by use of pictures.

Using all the information available, adults should be well placed to help promote the relationship between dog and child, and to inculcate desirable behaviour from both dog and child. In all of this, it is important that, where children are interacting with the dog, they are encouraged to do this in a way that is safe for them and for the dog. To achieve this, it might be that an older child can be encouraged to practise tasks such as feeding or grooming under the supervision of an appropriate adult, so that the dog is encouraged to see the child as someone they can rely on for positive attention and getting their needs met. Also, in terms of walking the dog in the garden, playing with the dog, or teaching him tricks, the child needs to be supported to do this assertively and sensibly. The Blue Dog Trust (www.thebluedog.org/en/) exists specifically to educate children in their relationship with dogs, and the child-friendly website contains a range of useful material.

Good practice example (from Kim Clark of Hertfordshire County Council Fostering Recruitment Team)

Hertfordshire Council was mindful that many of their foster carers owned dogs, but recognised that some of the looked after children were afraid of dogs or, because of their own experiences, could be aggressive and inappropriate around dogs. They had also experienced an unfortunate incident of a child being bitten by a dog in placement. Often the children did not understand how to behave around dogs, sometimes compounded by their experiences or because of specific conditions such as ADHD.

The adoption and fostering recruitment officer was familiar with a local and experienced dog training school as she had done some training with them, and had taken her own dog there. The owner was quite well known, having appeared on television programmes as an expert in dog training and behaviour, and it was decided that efforts should be made to develop links with this training school.

After some negotiations, Hertfordshire commissioned a number of sessions primarily for looked after children (but also for sons and daughters of foster carers), of different ages and needs, looking at dog safety, dog body language, and having fun with your dog. Feedback from the sessions was very positive, with foster carers noting that, in addition to being both enjoyable and educational for the children, they too had learned a lot.

Hertfordshire hopes to sustain the good relationship with the dog school in order for this arrangement to continue on an ongoing basis.

Good practice example (Blue Cross and Kent County Council)

Blue Cross offers free talks to parents and carers with young children under the title *Keeping your child safe around dogs*, and this was utilised by Gravesend's foster carer support group. Feedback from foster carers and supervising social workers was positive, and the content deemed very relevant to fostering.

The presentation aimed to help attendees to understand:

- the benefits of bringing up children with dogs

- dog welfare

- seeing things from the dog's point of view

- which boundaries are important and why

- understanding your dog's body language

- tips on keeping both child and dog happy and safe

To arrange this free talk, fostering services can email education@bluecross.org.uk or contact the Blue Cross education department on 0300 111 8950.

Chapter 5
Undertaking a dog assessment

This chapter of the guide is specifically linked to the CoramBAAF Dog Assessment Form (see Appendix A) and constitutes helpful guidance to foster carers, adopters and social workers regarding the completion of this form. An example of a completed assessment is contained in Appendix C.

THE ASSESSOR

Before undertaking a dog assessment, it is important that the assessor considers their own "cultural competence" to complete this task. Social workers need to have self-awareness of their own assumptions, values and biases that will impact on how they view the dog in a potential adoptive or foster home. For dog lovers, this will mean thinking carefully about safety and not making over-optimistic assumptions, and for those who dislike or fear dogs, it will mean being careful not to be overly critical or set too high expectations around issues such as safety and hygiene. In both cases, it is important to listen to the dog's owners, to remain mindful of what research tells us, and to use supervision to check out feelings and judgements.

THE CORAMBAAF DOG ASSESSMENT FORM

Basic details

As noted in Chapter 2, it is important to try and identify the breed of the dog to check that it is not categorised as a dangerous dog within the legislation, and to get some generalised information about the dog's likely temperament and behaviour. If the dog is a mongrel, this section should be used to describe the breeds that are thought to be part of the dog's heritage, although this will not be possible in all cases.

The age of the dog is important, in that puppies and younger dogs may be more unruly, boisterous and are still in the process of being trained. An older dog might be less able to cope with young children, may find any changes to routines more difficult, or be increasingly less amenable given the aches and pains of ageing. None of this should be assumed, however, but it will need to be considered.

The implications of whether the dog is neutered or not will also need discussion; if the dog has not been neutered, it will be important to know whether this has any relevance in terms of behaviour with people or with other dogs (see Chapter 4).

Personality and history

In considering the dog's personality, it will be necessary to rely largely on the owner's perspective, but this can be supplemented by observations from referees or the assessing social worker themselves. In describing personality, it can be useful to consider adjectives and phrases such as boisterous, placid, playful, possessive, nervous, aggressive, relaxed, submissive, protective of people, protective of property, obedient, and scared, although it is likely that the dog will respond differently in different contexts.

In considering the dog's history, state how the dog was acquired by the family: from a rescue centre, breeder, pet shop, family, friend, etc. Dogs acquired from rescue centres in particular may have experienced a history of ill-treatment, neglect or abandonment, and may exhibit behavioural difficulties as a result of that. This context might be important in terms of thinking about the dog's likely behaviour in certain situations, and careful consideration will need to be given to how a family might be able to manage a situation where both the dog and the child have an insecure pattern of attachment. Dogs from reputable breeders – the Kennel Club have an Assured Breeder Scheme – will come with known histories and characteristics, although sadly not all breeders are reputable.

It is also important to be clear about how long the dog has been with the family, and where the dog is a recent arrival then historical information is of even greater importance. If the dog has come from a rescue centre or been rehomed, it is important to know why. Dogs with persistent difficulties are often rehomed more than once, and a recently acquired dog may not yet have begun to show the problems that resulted in it needing to be rehomed previously. The Blue Cross (personal communication) suggests that, if prospective adopters or foster carers have a recently rehomed rescue dog, then they should allow at least three months for the dog to settle in, and for them to get to know their new dog.

Living arrangements, training and routines

In this section, the assessor needs to ask about practical arrangements, including which parts of the house, if any, the dog has access to. Specifically, it will be necessary to check on sleeping arrangements, as dogs need a safe place where they can be left in peace, free from children wanting to play with or pet them. It will also be helpful to find out about the dog's routines, particularly in relation to feeding and exercise, as the foster carer or adopter will need to consider how this can be managed in the context of also managing the needs of children.

The assessor will need to know whether the dog has attended formal training, either as a puppy or subsequently. It may be that the owners have instead offered informal training to their dog, but what matters most is that the dog is evidently under an appropriate level of control. The owner should be asked to describe whether the dog will follow basic commands and, if not, have considered the implications of this. The assessor should be able to confirm through informal observation whether the dog does in fact follow these commands and directions, or is otherwise managed.

Health and hygiene

Although the risk of infection from dogs is low, sensible hygiene procedures should be in place at all times, particularly if a crawling infant or toddler is likely to be placed. Most importantly, there should be proper arrangements to ensure that children, particularly young children, do not come into direct contact with dog faeces as this brings with it a number of health risks. This means that there will need to be appropriate arrangements for clearing up and disposing of any dog faeces from outside spaces that are accessible to children. Feeding arrangements should also be considered and deemed appropriate, recognising that there are a number of different perspectives about what dogs should eat and how they should be fed.

Dogs should all be registered with a vet, and it is advised (Dogs Trust, undated d; Blue Cross, 2012d) that they have three- or four-monthly routine preventative treatments for worms, fleas and lice. These treatments will reduce risk, particularly in households with younger and more vulnerable children, and where owners are not comfortable with such treatments, this will need further discussion.

The dog assessment form does ask about whether the dog is covered by health insurance or other arrangements. While it is not essential to have such cover, a responsible owner will have considered how they can secure medical treatment when their dog needs it.

Safety

The questions and checklist about safety are fairly self-explanatory, and attempt to identify whether there are potential concerns regarding the safety of the dog with children. Where concerns are identified, this will most likely lead to the need for a specialist dog assessment, but the social worker should use good judgement and common sense in interpreting the answers given. Although the checklist does require "yes/no" answers, the social worker is expected to use these as the basis for discussion, rather than automatically referring the matter for a specialist assessment.

Fostering panel chair

We turned down a couple at panel as their Rottweiler and German Shepherd had been trained as attack dogs, and the couple could not see any risks or problems with this. They said it was just for personal protection but the male applicant did some security work at night and it was suspected that he sometimes took a dog with him.

The dogs were trained to attack on a chain of trigger words but would also attack if the owners were attacked themselves, and the dogs would then release on command. The couple argued that because of the special commands, the dogs were guaranteed to respond, and there was no possibility at all of dogs attacking a child. We were not convinced by this argument and their complete lack of insight and denial of any risk compounded the panel's concerns.

The social work assessor had raised some concerns when she initially took on the assessment, but her manager had not supported her position. We requested a specialist assessment from an ex-police dog handler, but this was not sufficient to reassure the panel. In the end, we felt that the risks were simply too great.

Social worker's observations

While much of the information in the dog assessment form will inevitably be provided by the applicants, it is important that the social worker's observations reinforce what is being said in other parts of the form. They will be a regular visitor to the home and are well placed to take a view on the dog's temperament and the extent to which the dog follows the owner's commands. Where there are birth children in the home, the assessor will be able to observe their interaction with the dog, and may also choose to speak to the applicant's referees about their experiences of the dog, especially if they have any reason for concern.

Fostering manager

I came into a new post to find a situation with a foster carer and her dogs that was causing some concern within the service. The foster carer was approved to foster one child aged 0–5, and had five large dogs. A placement had recently ended when a parent had raised concerns about their child living with so many animals, and we needed to decide whether she continued to be suitable to foster.

I decided to undertake a visit myself. The foster carer lived on a new estate, and when I visited it was clear that the home was well presented and the dogs were well cared for, but nevertheless there was an overpowering smell of dogs and a litter of puppies had recently been born. The carer was approved for toddlers and babies, but if children had wanted to play on the floor they would have ended up covered in dog hair. Although I consider myself quite positive about dogs, I didn't think this environment was ideal for small children.

However, the most troubling issue for me was a sense from the foster carer that her primary motivation was caring for the dogs, and that the children's needs could be seen as secondary. Her lifestyle was geared very much to the dogs, and this could be problematic if the needs of a fostered child did not fit in with this. In short, I concluded that we should not place another child without specifically informing a parent about the number of dogs.

The assessing social worker should also make a common sense visual assessment of the dog in relation to any obvious concerns about their health or well-being. If the dog looks excessively thin, has sores, matted fur, or patches of missing fur, it would be appropriate to ask when the dog was last seen by a vet. In such a scenario, it would be entirely appropriate to ask for a report from the vet in relation to the animal's health and well-being. If a prospective foster carer or adopter is not looking after their dog appropriately, then this should raise concerns about whether they are suitable to care for vulnerable children.

Additionally, although there is expected to be one form completed for each dog in the family, where there is more than one dog the assessor will need to think about the interaction between them, and the implications of this for fostering or adoption. For example, there may be four extremely obedient and calm dogs together, or it may be that there are three dogs who individually are quite manageable, but excite each other causing a situation that could result in a child being hurt. The assessor will therefore need to be mindful of the dynamic between the animals, and the level of control that the owner has in this regard. It is generally easier to manage one slightly unruly dog than to manage three or four!

Social worker's summary and analysis

This is arguably the most important part of the report in that it brings together the other information and should reach a conclusion about whether the dog is clearly compatible with fostering or adoption, clearly incompatible, or whether further specialist input is required before reaching a definitive view.

Chapter 6
Specialist dog assessments

It is sometimes suggested that social workers lack the knowledge that is necessary to undertake a dog assessment, and that all assessments should be undertaken by a specialist in this area. Some fostering services use a specialist dog assessor for all dog assessments, and while this is not in itself problematic, it may be deemed overly bureaucratic and unnecessarily expensive. Some adoption agencies require prospective adopters to seek their own specialist dog reports from a suitably qualified person, and this is problematic in that it constitutes an unhelpful deterrent in the context of needing to maximise the number of potential adopters. This Good Practice Guide takes the position that dogs are commonplace in family homes, and in the vast majority of cases a well informed lay person will be able to make a judgement about safety, using common sense and the information provided in this guide.

That said, however, there clearly will be cases where more specialist input is required and it is recommended that fostering services and adoption agencies identify an appropriate person or persons who can undertake specialist assessments for them when needed. It is difficult to specify what qualification might be appropriate for this role (as training courses are not standardised or regulated) but it is important to look for a person with considerable understanding of dog behaviour and psychology, and experience of working with a range of dogs in a professional context. While some people might instinctively consider that a vet is most appropriate, it should be emphasised that it is not an understanding of health that is the key issue here. Often it is dog behaviourists, dog trainers or staff at dog rescue centres who are best placed to undertake this role; possible contacts are set out in Useful Organisations.

In considering whether to use a specialist dog assessor in a particular case, this needs to be a proportionate response, and as the result of specific identified concerns around safety. This might include factors such as the particular breed of dog, the history of the dog (including absence of history), or because of information that has arisen in the standard dog assessment. Often it will be because of a number of factors coming together. Where the assessing worker is concerned about any aspect of the dog's safety from what the applicant reports about the dog, from their personal experience during the assessment, or for other reasons, the fostering service or adoption agency should err on the side of caution and commission a specialist assessment.

Association of Pet Behaviour Counsellors (APBC): assessment for adoption and fostering placements

As the leading pet behaviour experts in the field, APBC members have been used by a number of agencies to assess animals and the homes of potential adoptive parents or foster carers. In response to demand, a standard protocol for use in this context has been developed and the APBC can now provide this service via a special network of participating full members. The service is designed primarily for dogs but may also be used for other animals. The assessment process involves:

- A visit to the home lasting approximately one-and-a-half hours.

- A report sent to the agency requesting the assessment, to include:

  - owner experience and relationship with the animal(s);

  - exposure and behaviour in various social situations, training background, and health issues;

  - practical considerations regarding the home environment;

  - temperament and behaviour with members of the household, visitors, general public, and children (0–5 years, 5–10 years, 10+ years);

  - a professional opinion on the risks these animals present to children, particularly those with social, emotional and behavioural difficulties.

- Advice regarding the introduction of children and animals.

The cost for this service is £120 plus mileage, at the discretion of the individual member providing the service in that area.

(https://www.apbc.org.uk/adoption-foster-assessments/)

A specialist dog assessment will need to be different from the standard assessment in a number of ways. Many assessors will undertake direct exercises with the dog in question, such as playing with him or her roughly and removing bones or toys to gauge the dog's response. The specialist assessor will also need to make a judgement about how the prospective adopter or foster carer handles and manages the dog; in terms of risk, this will be a crucial factor. Experienced individuals will have their own assessment methods and techniques, but it is crucial that their judgements remain relevant to the fostering and adoption task.

The assessment is not seeking to identify expert dog trainers, but rather ordinary people whose homes are sufficiently safe for children to live in.

Wherever a specialist dog assessor is commissioned, they should be required to provide a written report on their findings. While it would be unhelpful to stipulate the exact format for that report, it should include the concerns that prompted the report, the activity undertaken as part of the assessment, and the judgements reached by the assessor. It is often helpful if the assessor is able to grade the situation as low, medium or high risk, and make any recommendations about reducing the risk if appropriate.

Chapter 7
Dogs and placement

MATCHING

As indicated throughout this guide, the family dog needs to be considered as integral to the potential foster or adoptive family. At some point during the home study, the assessor will have explored the impact of a child joining the family and how this will be managed in relation to the family's existing routines and practices. Preparations, where needed, should have been implemented well before any child arrives, and this might have meant moving the dog's sleeping area to a quieter part of the house, or enclosing a "dog-free" area of the garden to allow babies and toddlers to play on the grass.

Most children who require foster care or adoption are already known to social workers, even if the admission to care takes place in an emergency. It is essential that information about the child is made available to the foster carers so that they can make an informed decision about whether the proposed placement will be likely to meet the child's needs. It needs to be established if the child has a history of allergies, is very afraid of dogs, has mistreated animals in the past, or has a cultural perspective that might impact on living with dogs in the new home. Where such information is not available, it might not be appropriate to progress with the placement, although this will need careful consideration.

It will, of course, be equally important that information about the dog is provided to the placing social worker, and to the child or young person. They should also have a choice about whether they are happy to live with a dog in the family, and the way that information is conveyed will depend in part on the amount of time available. In adoption and permanent fostering, it is anticipated that there will have been discussions about dogs at an early stage; for short-term or task-centred fostering placements, things will inevitably be less well planned.

Some fostering services and adoption agencies ask prospective foster carers and adopters to consider how they might respond if the combination of dogs and children proved untenable. In most cases, they are expecting the answer that the child will remain in placement and the dog will be re-homed, and in most cases this answer is given. For some people, this will be relatively easy if they have a relative or friend living nearby who is happy to take on the care of the dog, especially if that person already looks after the dog on occasions and has an existing relationship with the animal.

Case study: Boris

Boris, an eight-year-old West Highland Terrier, lived with foster carers who were approved as part of a multidimensional treatment foster care programme. Consideration was being given to placing a 12-year-old boy called Cameron with them.

Initially it looked like this would not be a good idea. Cameron's current placement was breaking down, in part because he insisted on constantly teasing the foster carer's puppy, and this was causing a high level of stress to the adults. Also, although a generally calm and good-natured dog, Boris had bitten one of the foster carer's teenage grandchildren on the toe when she had tried to push him outside using her bare foot. Notwithstanding these factors, this specialist placement potentially had a lot to offer Cameron, and the social worker was asked to undertake a risk assessment regarding the dog.

The issues identified above were on one side of the equation, but weighed against those risks there were other factors. Cameron had not been particularly aggressive towards the dog in his current placement, and to some degree the problem lay with the foster carers being arguably over-sensitive to the puppy's situation. Boris' owners were more laid back, and were also very confident and experienced carers who felt that they could manage the situation. Although Boris had bitten another child, he had been provoked, and even then he had "nipped"; it was not a serious injury that had needed hospital treatment. He was a mature dog who was usually very comfortable with children of all ages. It was also recognised that Cameron was particularly interested in dogs and needed to learn how to interact appropriately with them; avoidance was not going to be helpful in the longer term.

On the basis of the risk assessment, the placement was made and went extremely well. Cameron made huge gains from the treatment programme generally, and part of the reward structure was being allowed time to play with and care for the dog. By the end of the placement, Cameron had taken lead responsibility in the home for feeding, grooming and walking Boris.

However, for others it might not be that straightforward. It is easy to give the "correct" answer to a hypothetical question, and where fostering services require applicants to make this commitment to rehoming before they will approve them, the "correct" answer is even more likely. However, the reality might in fact be quite different. Some dog owners are incredibly attached to their four-legged family members, and the personal attributes that create this bond with the dog will likely be the same character traits that allow them to effectively bond with children in their care (Zilcha-Mano *et al*, 2011; Rockett and Carr, 2014). For these reasons, it is suggested that the effort should go into careful and effective matching, rather than trying to predict what might happen if things go wrong.

Emma (adopter)

We've recently adopted two children, and probably my biggest concern throughout the entire process was my dog! I think because I'd longed for children and tried for so long, he'd almost become a substitute child and I treated him more like a baby than a dog. Casper, a large German Shepherd, has always been very boisterous and he's fairly large, so even when we were first considering adoption, I was wondering how this would work.

When we were assigned our social worker for the home study, we were told that she was 'more of a cat person really, she expects dogs to sit and behave'. Eek!

Anyway, the home study part ended up being fine because our social worker largely ignored the dog. We had an official dog assessment, which I was very nervous about, but it was brilliant. The assessor was very friendly and experienced. He pulled and pushed the dog and did all the things children might do, like tugging his ears and stuff. He also gave us loads of fantastic advice about how to prepare Casper before the children arrived, such as getting him used to a new sleeping place, shutting him behind baby gates and the like. Casper passed with flying colours, which was a massive relief, but I was still a bit anxious about how he'd actually be when children moved in.

We were approved and looking for matches. We tended to check profiles to see if it mentioned that the children liked dogs. I was concerned that we'd get a child that would hurt him, as well as not being able to give him as much attention as he was used to. In our heads, we would tell ourselves that children come first, and we would rehome him if necessary, but looking back, I'm not sure if I would really have been able to.

We were matched with two very young children, aged one and two at placement. It was a long-distance placement, which meant that the plan was for Casper to go into kennels for three weeks (two weeks for introductions and a week for children to settle). I *almost* decided not to follow through with the match because of worries for the dog. He'd never been in kennels, the kids had had no contact with animals, and there would be no chance to introduce the kids before they came home. It was the worst possible situation really.

In the end, we took Casper to stay with my grandparents (some distance away), as I thought I'd feel happier during introductions if I could at least call up and check that he was OK. I did find I was able to focus on the children and put Casper to the back of my mind, which was a relief. However, I was quite worried about our son, as all through the introductions, all we saw him do was throw his toys everywhere, very hard too. I had visions of poor Casper trying to dodge a barrage of toy cars.

Despite all the worries, it's worked out brilliantly. After a week at home with just the children, my husband drove down to my grandparents to pick up Casper and bring him home again. I showed the children lots of pictures and told them that Casper was coming to live with us, just like they had. My son bonded with him straight away and my daughter adores him now. There were never any of the issues or problems I imagined. The only problem I have now is when both children and Casper all want to sit on my lap!

Overall though, I think Casper actually helped them settle and both children are always happy and excited to see him each morning. Casper himself adjusted really well too and is gentle with the children, even when they're yanking his ears or trying to "cuddle" him. He has learnt how to jump the baby gates which is a bit of an issue, but everything is way better than I expected it to be. I'm looking forward to the time when they're old enough to play together properly, as Casper will then get even more attention than he ever got before.

INTRODUCTIONS

Most foster carers and adopters will prepare books about their family to be used in matching and in preparing the child for placement. These books will include photographs of the house and garden, everyone who lives in the home, the local school, etc. It is important that the family dog is not omitted from this book, and that information is provided about how the dog is treated in the home, and what is acceptable and what is not. Some families have penned letters supposedly from their dogs to children prior to placement, or written the whole book from the perspective of the dog. This can allow for information and reassurances to be offered in a non-threatening and fun way.

Case study: Simba

One adoptive couple developed a family book for three girls they were hoping to adopt, using one of the family dogs as the author. The text, interspersed with photographs, ran as follows:

Hello, my name is Simba and I want to tell you about your forever family. This is Mum and Dad, but other people call them Sarah and Paul. I have lived with them since I was a small puppy and they have looked after me very well and loved me lots. Look at how small I was when I first came to live with Mum and Dad! Now I am two-and-a-half years old and much bigger. This is my sister Bluebell, but everyone calls her Bluey or Blue Dog. Bluey is three years old and has been living with us for nearly two years. Before that, she lived with different families and some of them did not look after her nicely. When she first came to us, she was worried that she might need to move again, but now she knows that she is part of our family. Also, Bluey is blind and so she does bump into people sometimes! Sometimes we are naughty [picture of Simba with muddy face] but Mum and Dad aren't cross with us for long and they always love us ...

The book goes on to describe, in words and pictures, the house and garden, including dog sleeping areas, local walks, schools, and local shops. Simba uses this opportunity to offer further reassurances to the children:

And this is my favourite shop ... the butchers! Me and Bluey's favourite food is meat, sometimes with a nice big bone ... We have lots of nice food in our house ... Sometimes we have treats. Me and Bluey have dog biscuits, and Mum and Dad like ice cream best. If you tell them your favourite food and treats, I'm sure they will get them for you.

The book then had photos of extended family and friends before Simba finishes with the words:

We're all looking forward to meeting you – are you good at throwing a ball?

Blue Cross (2012a, 2013a, 2014) offers specific and detailed advice in relation to preparing for babies and toddlers joining a dog-owning family, which emphasises the importance of early preparation and getting the dog ready for the new sounds and smells that come with children. Dog owners are also encouraged to prepare the dog for being handled by children, and to think about how the dog's need for exercise, attention and stimulation will continue to be met once children have joined the household.

When introducing the child and dog for the first time, some thought should be given to where and how that is best done. Dog owners will often know what is likely to work best with their dog, but Stilwell (2005, p 179) advises:

> Allow the dog to come up to you and sniff the top of your hand. If he doesn't want to come and greet you, leave him alone. Don't approach a dog from behind. Don't pet a dog directly on the top of its head. It could be threatening. Rub him on his chest instead.

This is broadly confirmed by Blue Cross (2012a):

> Help prevent your dog feeling overwhelmed by insisting the dog approach the children rather than the other way round. This prevents feelings of being under threat and your dog is less likely to snap in self-defence. Children can encourage the dog to come to them by sitting down and offering a titbit or a game with a toy. Ask them not to stare as this can be threatening. If the dog goes to them, they can stroke and fuss underneath the animal's chin to begin with rather than patting on the head. Remember, a dog at face level with young children may seem quite frightening, so be prepared to move the dog away if the child becomes overwhelmed or if the dog is about to jump up.

Introductions should never be made when a dog is sitting on their owner's lap as this can potentially be setting up a situation where the dog might feel that it is guarding its owner. Any particular plan will also need to be informed by what is known about the individual dog and children, and in most cases the owners will know from past experience how they can manage introductions in a way that works best for all parties.

Once the placement is made, adult vigilance is still required to ensure that both the child and dog remain safe. After an initial "honeymoon period", children can direct more challenging behaviour towards the new family, and this can extend to the canine family member as well.

DEALING WITH THE DEATH OF A DOG

There is always the possibility, particularly if placing a young child in a family with a mature dog, that the animal will die while the child is relatively young. Bereavement can be especially confusing for young children who may as yet have no concept of what death is and what happens when people or animals die, and where children have already suffered significant losses, this can be very difficult. The Dogs Trust (undated c) suggests that parents can help children in the following ways; this advice is equally applicable to foster carers and adopters:

- *Allow them to express their feelings and concerns. Try not to lose patience or treat their worries as trivial, and make it clear that they aren't the only ones feeling upset. Letting them know that you are also upset will reassure them that their feelings are justified and normal.*

- *Don't try and protect children too much; stick to truthful explanations, avoiding ideas of being "put to sleep" that can be misinterpreted, and lead to potential fears about sleep and death being connected.*

- *Reassure them that no one is to blame for the dog dying, least of all the child themselves.*

- *Try to involve older children in decisions about euthanasia and possibly with planning a memorial.*

- *Encourage them to talk about the dog and recall happy memories.*

- *Be sure to notify their teacher(s) when they go back to school so that they are aware of any differences in mood or attitude; they may also be able to offer support and a friendly ear.*

While the death of a much-loved dog is inevitably going to be difficult for both adults and children, sharing in the family grief can be an inclusive and unifying experience, and can even provide an opportunity for exploring past losses; all of which might help with assimilation into their new family (see example in Chapter 3). Issues about the death of a family pet are considered in more depth by Tuzeo-Jarolmen (2007) and elsewhere (see References and Useful Organisations). In particular, the Blue Cross (2012c) produces a very useful leaflet about supporting children around the death of a pet, and their Pet Bereavement Support Service operates a helpline.

Chapter 8
General principles in considering other pets

While 25 per cent of families in the UK own a dog, 45 per cent own a pet of some sort (PFMA, 2014), and so assessors should think about how other pets may impact on fostering and adoption. It is important to start by recognising that many of the benefits associated with dog ownership will often also apply with other animals.

> **Mary (social worker)**
>
> Many of our adopters and foster carers have a variety of pets: cats, dogs, guinea pigs, hamsters, rabbits, ducks, chickens and horses, to name but a few. Bearing in mind that many looked after children come from homes where pets may have been neglected or ill-treated, children can experience the positive side of caring for animals and on the whole clearly enjoy their company. If a child has been frightened by an animal that is without appropriate boundaries, or is out of control, this is also an opportunity for foster carers to help a child overcome their fears, which could mean that a child could later be placed in a family with such a pet, rather than miss out on a potentially good permanent placement.
>
> Children who have experienced trauma will frequently engage with, or respond to, animals rather than people in the early stages, as trusting a human will often take time. Many animals are soft and gentle and require no obvious reward, other than stroking or feeding, which children can learn as part of the nurturing process that foster care or adoption should provide. Pets can also be fun, relaxing and educational. When family finding for two individual children who lived with foster carers and their chickens, it was lovely to observe them feeding the birds, helping to clean their huts, and gathering eggs for their breakfast each day.

It is impossible to write a guide that would offer detailed information on all the different types of animals that might be owned by those who express an interest in fostering or adoption. However, there are a number of general principles that practitioners will need to apply in considering the issues that come with various types of animals.

- The psychological and physical health benefits to humans from keeping animals is well recognised in academic literature (O'Haire, 2010; Rockett and Carr, 2014) and needs to be seen as a potentially positive aspect of a foster or adoptive home (Thomas *et al*, 1999, pp 118–119).

- Attitudes to the ownership of different animals can be varied, and in relation to fostering and adoption it is important that practitioners are aware of their own feelings and prejudices. Only then will they be able to ensure that these are not getting in the way of evidence-based decision making.

- The safety of children is paramount, and should never be disregarded or treated lightly. Assessments in this regard should take account of general information about species or breeds but ultimately need to be based on the individual animal and their owners.

- The health risks associated with pets are generally low, and can usually be managed through appropriate hygiene measures. Babies and young children are at greater risk than older children because their immune systems are less developed, and this may also be true of children with certain health conditions.

- Issues of risk and safety should be balanced against the potential benefits of owning pets; it is neither possible nor desirable to completely eliminate risk from the life of a child.

- Any decisions or judgements need to be evidence-based, and assessing social workers should be sufficiently well informed. It is reasonable to expect that owners of unusual pets will be able to direct the assessor to relevant material, but the internet is another good source of basic information, if used with caution.

- In rare cases where a household contains an animal listed in the Dangerous Wild Animals Act 1976 (UK-wide legislation), registration with the local authority is required. In these circumstances, the assessing social worker should seek the applicant's permission to speak with the person responsible for agreeing the license.

- Where someone owns a potentially dangerous animal, especially where this is an unusual animal, or one used for specialist purposes such as horse-riding, then it should be expected that they have knowledge and expertise, especially in regards to safety issues.

- Where issues are complex, it may be helpful to make use of a specialist practitioner who is familiar with the animal in question, and who is briefed so that they have a basic understanding of the issues involved in fostering and adoption. However, in most circumstances it should not be necessary to involve a third party in the assessment.

- Careful matching will be necessary to ensure that meeting the needs of any children being placed will not be compromised by the animals living in the foster or adoptive home. This might be in relation to health issues such as allergies, or regarding the known behaviour of either the child or the animal.

- Consideration should also be given to the wishes and feelings of the child or young person and their birth family. Not everyone will feel comfortable with their child living in a household with a rat or snake.

- Assessing social workers should always make a common sense visual assessment of an animal in a foster home; if there are any indications of concern about the animal's health, then a check with a vet should be requested.

- Where social workers in the course of their work come across cases of (possible) animal cruelty or neglect, careful consideration should be given to referring the matter to the RSPCA or police.

PET ASSESSMENT FORM

A CoramBAAF pet assessment form (Appendix B) has been developed for use with a variety of animals, as it is not practical to develop separate assessment forms for each different species. An example of a completed cat assessment using this form is contained in Appendix D. Undertaking an assessment will require assessing social workers to use good judgement and provide relevant information according to the type of animal being considered. This will include deciding whether it is necessary to use the full pet assessment form or simply the space that is provided in section A of the Prospective Foster Carer Report (Form F) England (or equivalent in Scotland, Wales or Northern Ireland). Unlike the dog assessment form, where one form should be used for each animal, it might be appropriate to use a single pet assessment form for a group of animals of the same species or type. Again, this will be a matter of judgement.

While some of the information that has been provided in relation to dogs will be applicable in relation to other pets, there will also be specific issues that need to be considered, depending on the particular type of animal, and these are considered in the following chapters.

Chapter 9
Cats

Cats are actually more common in family homes than dogs, but the issues are usually less complex. While cats will generally be less likely to cause an injury to a child, they do scratch, and some cats will be more aggressive and less comfortable with human contact than others. These aspects of personality will need to be considered and, where appropriate, prospective foster carers and adopters will have to think about how they might manage the challenges that this could potentially bring.

Issues of health and hygiene will also need consideration. Much of this will be similar to the issues identified in terms of dogs (see discussion of toxocariasis in Chapter 3), and most vets will recommend regular vaccinations and boosters as well as preventative treatment of worms, lice and fleas. It should be noted that, unlike most dogs, cats are inclined to jump onto work surfaces and some cats will bring in birds and rodents from the garden, and this will need to be managed to maintain appropriate hygiene. Toileting arrangements must be considered and information provided about how this might be dealt with in a way that ensures the good health of any children in the family.

Specifically in the consideration of cats, there is the issue of toxoplasmosis, an infection caused by a common parasite often found in their faeces, which can be transmitted by the consumption of food, water or soil infected by the cat faeces (NHS, 2013a). Estimates suggest that up to a third of the UK population will acquire a toxoplasmosis infection at some point in their life, but most people will not notice any symptoms. Toxoplasmosis can be more serious in people with weakened immune systems such as babies and young children.

Severe congenital toxoplasmosis occurs when a woman becomes infected during pregnancy and passes the infection on to her unborn baby. This can result in the baby developing serious health problems, such as brain damage and partial blindness. Ocular toxoplasmosis is another possible and serious complication where the infection spreads to the eyes, leading to partial or complete loss of vision (NHS, 2013a).

However, the NHS (2013a) and the Centers for Disease Control and Prevention (2013) note that there are a number of measures you can take to help reduce the risk of developing a toxoplasmosis (or toxocariasis) infection, and these are basic good hygiene practices:

- Wear gloves when gardening, particularly when handling soil, and wash your hands thoroughly afterwards with soap and hot water.

- Wear gloves when changing a cat's litter tray and wash your hands thoroughly afterwards.

- Wash fruit and vegetables before eating them.

- Change cat litter trays daily as it takes at least 24 hours for the toxoplasma parasite to become infectious.

NHS (2013a) and CDC (2013) additionally suggest that owners feed their cat 'dried or canned food rather than raw meat', and offer advice to cat owners about the need to 'wash all kitchenware thoroughly after preparing raw meat'. However, the same logic presumably requires that people do not prepare raw meat for their own consumption, and so this advice will need to be considered in that light.

The Cats Protection website has useful information, including some that is specifically designed to be accessible to children, and some specifically about cats and babies. The key elements of the latter (Cats Protection, 2012) include the following:

- Never leave the baby and cat alone together.

- Never leave a child's sand box uncovered as the cat may use this as a litter tray.

- Ensure that the cat remains in good health, is treated for worms and fleas, and is neutered.

- Ensure proper hygiene with cat litter trays, and keep cat food and baby food separately.

- Use a safe cot or pram net and don't let the cat climb on nursery furniture or prams.

- Provide a high-up place where cats can observe what is happening but be out of reach.

- Set aside part of your day to make a fuss of the cat so that they do not feel neglected.

Matching will of course be important, as children might be allergic to cats (NHS, 2012), although it should be noted that Cats Protection (2012) provides some helpful information about allergies and how to manage these.

An example of a completed cat assessment using the CoramBAAF pet assessment form is contained in Appendix D.

Megan (adopter)

When my two-year-old son was placed with me, I already had a cat, Eric, that I had had from a little kitten. In fact, my son and the cat are almost the same age, born within a few weeks of each other! I was a bit worried about how Eric would react as he had been used to just me and my parents and hadn't had much contact with children, and was still quite young. So, prior to the placement I moved him temporarily to my parents' home, which was close by.

My son had been used to pets in his foster placement and was keen to meet Eric. We told him that Eric was shy and so we had to be gentle with him; we visited him, and we took him some treats. After about a week Eric had stopped hiding when my son ran in, but rather was following him around waiting for his treat. When they were able to sit on my lap together, we decided to bring the cat back to our home.

We had a day where together we set up everything for the cat, then went and got him and brought him to our house. We compared it to my son coming to his new home and finding his way around and getting settled in. In fact, I often compare them, as both had birth mothers that couldn't manage, meaning that they went to temporary homes until their "forever mummy" was found for them.

It probably only took about two or three weeks before Eric seemed totally happy and my son had stopped trying to entice him over every time he came into the room and would just let him be. My son now feeds the cat each day, plays with him, hugs him, tells him off and explains everything to him. The cat patiently sits and listens if he reads a book to him.

Eric is happily settled and seems very comfortable with my son, will let him stroke him, will sit or lie next to him, but won't let him dress him up! Also, he won't let my son pick him up, but since Eric is huge I'm not sure that my son would get him off the ground! Eric is quite happy to show you if he has had enough and will give a nip or swipe, but he does it rarely and it's usually deserved. I consider that my son has to learn not to do things that the cat can't tolerate. I'm really happy with how they have settled, and they look adorable when the cat curls up next to him in bed.

Sheila (adopter)

The assessment of the cats was a combination of my social worker observing them and me completing a four-page pet questionnaire. From memory, some of the questions were:

- *How often are they groomed and by whom?* I found this one a bit silly for cats, but apparently I made some of the panel giggle at my response: they lick themselves daily, sometimes hourly.

- *What would I do if they injured my child?*

- *Could anyone verify that they are healthy and in good condition?* My vets can as they see them at least twice a year.

- *Were their injections up to date and could I prove it?* I could, as I have their certificates.

One thing that was asked at the panel was if I was aware that cats sometimes smother babies. I was and had already bought a cat cot net in anticipation. Rather strangely, I was also asked how I would keep them out of a child's bedroom; the answer I gave is the very obvious one – shut the door!

In terms of introductions, I started with including the cats in the talking photo album that my son got after matching panel approval. He was already able to point to the cats in the album by the time I met him for the first time. I also did some safety-proofing of the house with stair gates and the like, so that the cats could get up and down the stairs for a bit of an escape. I also changed where their food is stored so that my son couldn't access it.

About midway through introductions, I brought home a worn babygro so that the cats could sniff it and get used to his smell. One of them slept on it the first night and getting the cat hair out of it was a nightmare! But it seems to have helped the cats adjust as they already knew what he smelt like.

Since placement, we've all got into an easy routine. I feed the cats when my son is eating breakfast or napping so that they can eat in peace, and I've moved their water bowl from the bottom of the stairs to behind the stair gate as my son thought it was his own private paddling pool! The cats are slowly getting braver and only run away now if he chases them. There's also been a couple of successful cat stroking sessions – it works best when my son is calm and a bit tired (so just before bed is ideal). The main challenge at the moment is his shrieking, which petrifies the cats and sends them running for cover ...

Fostering manager

As a manager who had recently moved to a new local authority, I was supervising an assessing social worker in my team. After reading the first draft of a fostering assessment, I fed back that there had been no assessment or discussion about the two cats in the home, and also raised some concerns about the ability of the couple to work with others. There were hints that both aspects might be problematic. I suggested further discussion with the applicants and then further reflective consideration with me regarding our recommendation.

A few weeks later, when I returned from a weeks' leave, I was surprised to find that the case had been presented at the panel, without my having signed it off, and with a recommendation and decision that the couple were suitable to foster. A 10-year-old boy had already been placed!

Unfortunately, my initial concerns were proved valid. After a few weeks, the fostering service received a telephone call saying that the carers wanted the placement to end because the boy was pestering the cats. One of the foster carers was saying that the cats were her babies, and that 'no one messes with them'. She insisted that she had told the assessor this. The carer was clearly agitated, angry at the boy in placement, and threatening to 'throw him across the room' if he touched the cats again.

It was decided that the placement needed to end; it was clearly not a nurturing or even safe arrangement. As a result of not undertaking a proper pet assessment, the boy had a further – and unnecessary – placement move.

Chapter 10
Snakes and reptiles

Snakes and reptiles, like dogs and other pets, can bring potential benefits to the foster home in terms of education, leisure interests and learning about responsibility for other living things. But like dogs, and potentially even more so, there are a range of human responses to reptiles, many of them adverse, and social workers will need to be careful that their own perspectives do not unfairly impact on their judgements.

Where snakes, reptiles or insects are venomous, then safety is obviously of crucial importance. Guidance is provided by the Environment and Heritage Service Northern Ireland (EHSNI, undated) including that:

> Snakes must be housed in locked tanks (vivaria) kept inside a locked room. The room housing the reptiles must be "snake proof" to prevent accidental escape. Venomous lizards may be kept in vivaria or fine mesh wire cages with a solid floor.

Such advice may also be relevant in relation to snakes and other reptiles that are not venomous, but nevertheless need to be kept safely and securely. Keeping venomous animals will require registration under the Dangerous Wild Animals Act 1976, and the person granting the license will need to be involved in considering whether this is compatible with fostering or adoption. Safety will also be important in relation to any larger powerful snakes such as boa constrictors and pythons where the risk might relate to constriction rather than bites.

Any assessment will need to look at feeding arrangements, and in some cases there may be an issue about snakes being fed on live prey such as mice and rats. There is some lack of clarity around the legality of this practice, but DEFRA (in private correspondence) note that while it is not expressly prohibited under the Animal Welfare Act 2006 (England and Wales), it might contravene sections of that Act insofar as it could be deemed to cause an animal unnecessary suffering or could fail to comply with requirements for good welfare practices. The RSPCA agrees.

> Feeding live prey to captive animals may be viewed as illegal under the provisions of the Animal Welfare Act 2006 if the prey's needs are not being met. Apart from the distress caused to live prey, the predator itself can be damaged in the process of catching and ingesting the prey.

(RSPCA, undated)

For these reasons, there is much advice online to snake owners to feed their pets on dead rather than live rodents, including advice on how to encourage this if the snake is reluctant. Where a potential foster carer or adopter insists on live feeding, it would be necessary to understand why they are ignoring advice about the well-being of both predator and prey. This is an emotive subject and will need careful consideration. Feeding live insects such as crickets, locusts and worms of various sorts is not covered by this legislation, and while some might find this uncomfortable, it is generally accepted to be a less controversial practice.

From a health perspective, there is also a particular issue that needs to be considered regarding salmonella, helpfully set out in the following information from Public Health England (2011):

Salmonella are bacteria found in the gut of many animals, including reptiles. The bacteria can spread from the animals to cause illness in people. Though salmonella infection in people usually causes a mild illness with fever, vomiting, abdominal pain and diarrhoea, more severe illness can occur. Babies, children under five, pregnant women, the elderly and those with weaker immune systems are particularly at risk from infection ... and are more likely to develop serious illness, which can be fatal.

Most reptiles carry salmonella in their gut without showing any signs of infection and shed the bacteria in their droppings. These droppings can quickly spread over the reptile's skin, and any surface or object that the reptile comes into contact with can be contaminated with salmonella, including cages, toys, clothes, furniture, and household surfaces.

Salmonella can pass from reptiles to people when people put anything in their mouth that has come into contact with their reptile – particularly their fingers. Some reptile foods such as frozen or defrosted mice, rats and chicks, can also contain salmonella and be a potential source of infection for both the reptile and its owners.

Children are particularly at risk because they like to handle and stroke pet reptiles. As a result, their hands and fingers can become contaminated. Babies and small children may be infected by parents and other family members who have handled a reptile and then not washed their hands before feeding or touching the child. They may also become infected from reptile droppings if the reptile is free to roam the home.

Good care of your reptile will reduce the risks of salmonella infection. It is not possible to eliminate salmonella from reptiles. Below are some important guidelines on how to reduce the risk of catching salmonella from your reptile.

- *Always supervise children to ensure that they do not put your reptile (or objects that the reptile has been in contact with) near their mouths, and wash their hands immediately after [contact].*

- *Keep your reptile out of rooms where food is prepared and eaten, and limit the parts of the house where your reptile is allowed to roam freely.*

- *Always wash your hands thoroughly with soap and water immediately after handling your reptile, their cage or any other equipment such as soaking pools.*

- *Always wash your hands thoroughly with soap and water immediately after feeding your reptile, and after handling raw (frozen or defrosted) mice, rats or chicks. Ensure that all surfaces that have come into contact with defrosting food are cleaned thoroughly afterwards.*

- *Do not eat, drink or smoke while handling your reptile.*

- *Do not kiss your reptile.*

- *Do not use kitchen sinks to bathe your reptile or to wash their cage or equipment. If you use a bathroom sink or bathtub, it must be cleaned thoroughly with disinfectant afterwards.*

- *Dispose of waste water and droppings from your reptile down the toilet instead of a sink or bathtub.*

With these considerations in mind, fostering services and adoption agencies will need to consider how they respond to applicants who have reptiles as pets. Some more cautious websites do suggest that reptiles are unsuitable pets for families with babies and small children. Given the fact that babies and children under five are most vulnerable to salmonella, fastidious hygiene measures will be necessary if keeping reptiles as pets is going to be compatible with caring for this group of children. The assessing social worker will need to be confident that any risk will be reduced to a level that is acceptable, and, particularly with these most vulnerable children, the onus should be on the applicants to explain how their situation is sufficiently safe.

In considering these matters, it is necessary to achieve a balance that understands the real issues around health risk and reptiles, but also takes account of the fact that many children live safely and happily in households with reptile pets. With older children and sensible hygiene practices, fostering or adoption should be perfectly possible for people owning reptiles.

Chapter 11
Other pets

FISH

There are more fish kept as pets in the UK than any other animals, and while on the one hand it might seem unnecessary to undertake a pet assessment regarding pet fish, there are some important issues to consider. Although the animals themselves present no risk, it will be necessary to think about risks arising from young children getting into fish tanks, crashing into them because of where they are placed, or pulling them down on top of them. Lucas (2012) advises:

> Never set your tank up in a high traffic area. If someone happens to trip and fall, they can easily break the tank, getting badly cut by the broken glass. If you hope to place a tank in a high traffic area or buy one for small children, consider one of the acrylic tanks. Plastic is much safer in these circumstances.

The chemicals used for things like water purification and cleaning must also be stored safely and away from small children, and Lucas (2012) notes that salmonella can breed in fish tanks so careful hand washing is important. Where fish are kept outside in a pond, the assessor will need to be reassured about children's safety from drowning, although this will in any case be addressed as part of the general home safety check.

Mary (social worker)

Tropical fish can be very relaxing and calming to observe. A little girl I know went straight to the tank on her very first visit to her adopter's home and often sits mesmerised by the brilliant colours and the way they move. She now enjoys swimming like a fish at the local pool, having previously been frightened by water.

On the other hand, I recall visiting some prospective adopters who could not accept that a six-foot deep koi carp tank in their garden posed a potential risk to children and would need some form of grid to provide security. Needless to say, we did not progress this assessment.

The strangest experience was when I spotted a fish tank in the living room at the beginning of a visit but became increasingly aware of a lack of movement. It became clear that in fact there were plastic fish suspended in the tank; they were cheaper, and easier to clean!

BIRDS

There are a number of birds that people keep as pets and it will be necessary to think about what may need to happen to prevent children from being bitten, as well as ensuring appropriate hygiene arrangements. Cohen (2013) acknowledges that birds can carry diseases that can be transferred to humans but suggests that this is manageable:

For the average pet owner, a few simple precautions and hygiene practices should significantly lower the risk of any zoonotic infections. These include always thoroughly washing hands with soap after handling the pet, disinfecting the bird's cage, food bowls and toys on a regular basis, never allowing the bird near food preparation areas and not cleaning any bird-related items in the kitchen sink or bathroom sink, where family members are likely to be preparing food or washing themselves. If a separate utility sink is not available, then make sure to always disinfect the sink thoroughly after use. Most of all, discourage any family members from kissing the bird on the lips!

Cohen (2013) provides considerable further advice including how to minimise risk when purchasing a bird, and particularly with larger species like parrots and macaws recommends annual checks with a specialist bird vet. Some may consider that to be excessively cautious, but at the very least, owners should be alert to any signs of respiratory illness or poor condition in the bird, and seek urgent advice in these circumstances.

Public Health England (2012, 2014) provides specific information about psittacosis (also known as parrot fever), an infection most commonly found in parrots, parakeets, budgerigars and cockatiels. This can be transmitted to humans, and domestic bird contact is considered to be responsible for a significant number of the 50 or so cases reported in England and Wales each year. Psittacosis typically causes respiratory problems and influenza-like symptoms, but can lead to severe pneumonia and health problems. Symptoms will often be mild or moderate, but certain population groups with less developed or compromised immune systems, including young children, will be more vulnerable.

Transmission of psittacosis occurs mainly through inhalation of airborne matter such as respiratory secretions, dried faeces or feather dust, but

Fiona (adopter)

We have adopted siblings who were aged four and two, and when the children moved in we had dogs, cats, over 50 chickens, 20 ducks and two geese. The kids loved them all. My son is now inseparable from the youngest dog; they walk around together and he kisses the dog and says 'Wuv you', which is just adorable.

When the children joined us it was quite life-changing, as we all had to get to know each other, and this included the pets. The children needed routine, structure and boundaries, and helping to look after the pets became an activity that we did together. We showed them how to care for the pets, to interact with them, and to get joy out of them. They helped me with feeding, grooming and cleaning out the birds' living areas. Playing with and caring for the pets helped us all bond and kept us smiling.

Having birds, dogs and cats, there were obvious safety and hygiene risks so we made sure that the children were never alone with any of the animals and that they fully understood how to play, stroke and take care of them. The dogs are very placid but both children have learnt never to pull or pinch them or play rough. The geese especially can nip and the children are now fully aware of this and take caution when in the field or near the geese. From a hygiene perspective, the children were taught not to touch bottoms or poo and to wash their hands after playing with the animals, as well as not putting their fingers in their mouths.

Unfortunately, we had a spate of fox attacks and it became evident that the foxes were winning the battle with the birds. So, gradually and sensitively we began to rehome the chickens and ducks, educating the children on how important it was that the birds were happy rather than being attacked by a fox. The kids knew where the birds were moved to, and that they now have their own pond, and some ponies and sheep to play with.

transmission is also possible through oral infection and handling of infected birds. Public Health England (2012) offers advice about reducing the likelihood of infection, including:

- regular cleaning of cages, ensuring that faeces do not accumulate for long enough to dry out and become airborne;

- cleaning food and water bowls daily using soap, water and disinfectant solution;

- use of litter on the bottom of the cage that will not produce dust, such as newspaper.

The matching process will need to take account of the fact that children can have allergies associated with living in close proximity to birds, or that this can trigger asthma (NHS, 2012).

RABBITS AND RODENTS

Assessments regarding rabbits and rodents will need to be proportionate to both the animal and the situation, but it is important that adopters and foster carers have thought through how they will manage the issues according to the age of the child or children envisaged, and the particular circumstances of their household. For example, if birth children are responsible for looking after a pet rabbit or rodent, then how would foster children be included in this, and what measures might be needed to ensure that children can only access the animals when they are being appropriately supervised?

It also needs to be recognised that individual animals may behave in different ways, and some rabbits, for example, depending on their temperament and experience, can kick and scratch if they feel frightened or uncomfortable. All rabbits and rodents can bite and, with small children in particular, contact will need to be supervised at all times. Depending on the type of animal and the specific individual, it may be sufficient to include written information within the body of the assessment report rather than using a separate pet assessment form. This will be a judgement for the assessing social worker.

HORSES

Relationships between humans and horses can be particularly strong, and especially where horses are kept for riding, this can bring enormous benefits to children in foster or adoptive homes. The therapeutic benefits of riding and caring for horses are well recognised, and the following quotes from Gilligan (2009, pp 71–73) serve to illustrate such benefits.

His latest activity is horse-riding. We often got complaints from school about how he could not sit still and concentrate for more than a brief moment. Miraculously, he can sit on a pony for over an hour and just move as necessary. It's incredible to see the concentration and work he can apply on horseback. The feeling of the big animal so close and the whole process of sitting and riding seems to work wonders at any age and for almost any child. He looks forward [to it] every week and is slowly but surely becoming more confident.

'I used to go up to the horse about six o'clock, you know. The big red sun would be there, you know, and a beautiful day out ... I'd go up and she would be knackered, you know, after she's been running around with other horses all day and I'd go up to her and the second I'd touch her, she's gone, she's out for the count and I'd rub her and rub her and rub her and talk to her. It was a straightforward bond with that horse. It was like we had something going. If someone was annoying me I'd go up to the horse. I'd rather tell them than hurt anyone else. I'd tell me horse before I'd tell me old ma, you know what I mean?'

So if prospective foster carers or adopters own horses, this will potentially be of great benefit to children in their care, but there are of course risks involved, and safety will need to be considered. It is not appropriate for this guide to set out all the issues, as they are complex and quite specific, but the owners should be able to reassure the assessing social worker that they are aware of the potential risks and how to manage these. They should be able to explain some of the rules that they will need to convey to children, and be able to talk authoritatively about horses in general, and the specific personality of their horse or horses in particular. They will also have needed to consider the issue of safety in relation to the stables or wherever they keep their horse. It will of course be easier to assess this matter where the owners already have children riding or caring for the horse, as they will be able to talk from experience about how they managed this. The British Horse Society (2010) and Blue Cross (2012b) provide helpful information about safety and horse ownership.

Where children are involved with riding horses, especially on the road, there is always the risk of injury or of third party claims, and a responsible horse owner should ensure that third party liability insurance cover is in place. Fostering services and adoption agencies might reasonably expect this. There are several membership organisations that provide rider insurance, and the child could have the benefit of being a member of the club as well, with minimal outlay.

FARM ANIMALS

Although farm animals are not usually pets, it will be necessary for assessments of farmers and others who keep livestock to consider any implications that this might have in respect of fostering and adoption. While farmers routinely bring up their birth children without concern, it might be different if, for example, foster children are unused to living in a farm setting, and where they may have behavioural issues that need to be considered. Assessments in relation to this will relate more to the general safety check of the accommodation than to the specific animals in question.

The Health and Safety Executive (HSE) produces a very informative document (HSE, 2013) about preventing accidents to children on farms.

In other circumstances, individuals may keep animals like goats as pets (see Buttercups Sanctuary in Useful Organisations) and assessments will need to be undertaken using the general principles set out above, taking into account that these types of animals must be kept in appropriate settings that can fully accommodate their needs.

Mary (social worker)

When assessing a family who kept pigs for their meat, we spoke about how they would explain this process to a child. They were used to giving their pigs names and their birth child was very accepting of the process which was clearly educational for her, as well as economical for the family. We have since placed a child with them who is just as enamoured with a different set of pigs, since their predecessors have ended up as chops, joints and sausages in their freezer. In the company of her sister, the adopted child is learning about the care of such animals and knows that the pigs will eventually be eaten for dinner. Children can be very accepting of simple explanations.

Chapter 12
Conclusion: developing local policies

All fostering services and adoption agencies should have policies regarding dogs and other pets. It will be for each to individually decide on the content of those policies, but the following guidance in relation to dogs may be helpful.

- Dogs can bring a number of positive aspects to a foster or adoptive home, and this needs to be recognised alongside any risks or problematic aspects.

- In making decisions about dogs, it is unhelpful to have overly rigid policies that fail to take into account the individual circumstances in any particular case. Any policy that relies on information about breed without considering the individual animal and circumstances risks being fundamentally flawed.

- Where prospective foster carers or adopters own dogs that are listed and/or registered under the Dangerous Dogs Act, this will usually be deemed incompatible with fostering or adoption, notwithstanding the considerable flaws in this legislation.

- Where dogs have been trained or used as guard dogs then, depending on the individual circumstances, it may be that this will be incompatible with fostering or adoption, and will certainly need very careful individual consideration involving a specialist dog assessor.

- In certain situations, it will be appropriate to involve a specialist dog assessor in considering the suitability of a particular dog in relation to fostering and adoption. This might relate to factors such as the particular breed, an unknown history, where the dog has had limited interaction with children, or most likely a combination of factors that have raised concerns.

- Fostering services and adoption agencies should identify locally based dog assessment specialists and ensure that they are trained to understand the issues in fostering and adoption. Arrangements should be in place to commission reports from them as required, with an agreed format for those reports.

- Fostering services and adoption agencies should expect that owners have carefully considered whether or not to neuter their dog, and are mindful of any behavioural implications of this.

- Dog owners should consider the benefits of routine annual inoculations and the use of regular treatments for worms and fleas. This is especially important if they are caring for babies or young children.

- Thorough matching is essential and full information needs to be taken into account about the child needing the placement and the dog, including the dog's role and position in the family.

- Where social workers, in the course of their work, come across cases of (possible) animal cruelty or neglect, careful thought should be given to referring the matter to the RSPCA or police.

Fostering services and adoption agencies may also wish to incorporate into their policies the general principles about other animals that are set out in Chapter 8.

Issues with dogs and other animals can bring considerable challenges to practitioners involved with fostering and adoption, and social workers often feel that they lack the skills required to deal with this aspect of the work. It is hoped that this practice guide has offered information, including a structured approach to assessment, such that these issues become less daunting.

While understanding that dogs and other pets can constitute a risk to children living in foster and adoptive homes, and that there is never room for complacency, it is important not to become overly focused on this element alone. Sensible measures can minimise these risks and the childhood of many people has been enriched by the companionship and unreserved love of a dog or other pet. This is no different for children in foster and adoptive homes.

References

Association of Pet Behaviour Counsellors (APBC) (2012) *APBC's Guide to Dog Safety for Children and Parents*, available at: www.apbc.org.uk/info/dog_safety_information

Association of Pet Behaviour Counsellors (APBC) (2013a) *Neutering Risks and Benefits: Bitches*, available at: www.apbc.org.uk/wp-content/uploads/APBC-Neutering-Male-Dogs.pdf

Association of Pet Behaviour Counsellors (APBC) (2013b) *Castration Risks and Benefits: Dogs*, available at: www.apbc.org.uk/system/files/private/summary_sheet_of_castration_risks_and_benefits.pdf

Blue Cross (2012a) *Introducing your Dog to the Family*, available at: www.bluecross.org.uk/pet-advice/introducing-your-dog-family

Blue Cross (2012b) *Safety around Horses*, available at: www.bluecross.org.uk/pet-advice/safety-around-horses

Blue Cross (2012c) *Missing my Friend: Support for children*, available at: www.bluecross.org.uk/pet-loss-support-children-missing-my-friend

Blue Cross (2012d) *Basic Healthcare*, available at: www.bluecross.org.uk/pet-advice/basic-healthcare-dogs

Blue Cross (2013a) *Your Dog and your Baby*, available at: www.bluecross.org.uk/pet-advice/how-keep-your-baby-safe-around-your-dog

Blue Cross (2013b) *Your Cat and your Baby*, available at: www.bluecross.org.uk/pet-advice/how-introduce-your-cat-your-baby

Blue Cross (2014) *Keeping your Toddler Safe around Dogs*, available at: www.bluecross.org.uk/pet-advice/keeping-your-toddler-safe-around-dogs

British Horse Society (2010) *Reporting of Equestrian Incidents*, available at: www.horseaccidents.org.uk/Advice_and_Prevention/What_To_Wear/Headwear.aspx

Burgoyne1, Dowling L, Fitzgerald A, Connolly M, Browne J and Perry I (2014) 'Parents' perspectives on the value of assistance dogs for children with autistic spectrum disorder: a cross sectional study', *British Medical Journal Open*, 2014:4, available at: http://bmjopen.bmj.com/content/4/6/e004786.full

Cats Protection (2012) *Cats and Kids*, available at: www.cats.org.uk/uploads/documents/The_Cat_Mag_extracts/Cats_and_babies.pdf

Centers for Disease Control and Prevention (CDC) (2013) *Parasites: toxoplasmosis*, available at: www.cdc.gov/parasites/toxoplasmosis/prevent.html

Child Alert (2014) *Child Safety Advice and Statistics*, available at: www.childalert.co.uk/safety.php?tab=Safety

Cohen H (2012) *Dangerous Pet Diseases which can Infect Kids*, available at: www.saferpets.co.uk/dangerous-pet-diseases-which-can-infect-kids.html

Cohen H (2013) *Common Diseases from Pet Birds and How to Avoid them*, available at: www.saferpets.co.uk/diseases-from-birds-avoid.html

Dangerous Dogs Act Study Group (DDASG) *Submission from the Dangerous Dogs Act Study Group*, available at: http://archive.scottish.parliament.uk/s3/committees/lgc/inquiries/ControlofDogs/DDASG.pdf

Dietz T, Davis D and Pennings J (2012) 'Evaluating animal assisted therapy as group treatment for child sexual abuse', *Journal of Child Sexual Abuse*, 21:6, pp 665–683

Department for Education (2011) *The Children Act 1989 Guidance and Regulations: Fostering services*, London: HMSO

Dogs Trust (2010) *Dog Behaviour Problems*, available at: www.dogstrust.org.uk/help-advice/behaviour/

Dogs Trust (2011) *Research to Support the Canine Charter for Human Health,* available at: www.dogstrust.org.uk/az/d/dogprescription/theresearch.docx

Dogs Trust (2013) *A New Baby and the Family Dog*, available at: www.dogstrust.org.uk/help-advice/training/preparing-your-dog-for-a-new-baby

Dogs Trust (2014) *It's Nicer to Neuter*, available at: www.dogstrust.org.uk/help-advice/neutering/its-nicer-to-neuter-heres-why

Dogs Trust (undated a) *Staying Safe with Dogs*, available at: www.dogstrust.org.uk/help-advice/factsheets-downloads/stay%20safe%20around%20dogs.pdf

Dogs Trust (undated b) *Allergies*, available at: www.dogstrust.org.uk/az/a/allergies/#.VCQ5WPldXco

Dogs Trust (undated c) *Children and Bereavement*, available at: http://www.dogstrust.org.uk/az/b/bereavement/bereavementchildren09.aspx#.VCQ55PldXcp

Dogs Trust (undated d) *Worms, Ticks and Fleas*, available at: www.dogstrust.org.uk/az/h/healthproblems/vaccinationsandfleas.aspx#.VCQ6QvldXcp

Dogs Trust (undated e) *Dangerous Dogs Act*, available at: www.dogstrust.org.uk/news-events/issues-campaigns/dangerous-dogs/dangerous-dogs-the-original-situation

Environment and Heritage Service Northern Ireland (EHSNI) (undated) *Guidance on the Keeping of Venomous Snakes and Lizards*, available at: www.daera-ni.gov.uk/sites/default/files/publications/doe/natural-guidance-keeping-venomous-snakes-lizards.PDF

Gilligan R (2009) *Promoting Resilience*, London: BAAF

Gove M (2012) Speech on adoption, 23 February, available at: www.gov.uk/government/speeches/michael-gove-speech-on-adoption

Health and Safety Executive (2013) *Preventing Accidents to Children on Farms*, available at: www.hse.gov.uk/pubns/indg472.pdf

Kennel Club (2009) *Dangerous Dogs Act: A dog is only as good as its owner*, available at: www.thekennelclub.org.uk/media/24850/ddasg_4pp_bro_briefing_lores.pdf

Kennel Club Breed Information Centre (undated) available at: www.thekennelclub.org.uk/services/public/breed/Default.aspx.

Khanom M (2012) *Guide for Foster Carers caring for Muslim Children*, London: Mercy Mission

Lucas T (2012) *Freshwater Fish Safety*, available at: www.saferpets.co.uk/FreshwaterFishSafety.html

McConnell A, Brown C, Shoda T, Stayton L, and Martin C (2011) 'Friends with benefits: on the positive consequences of pet ownership', *Journal of Personality and Social Psychology*, 101: 6, pp1239–1252

Milan C (2008) *Cesar's Way*, London: Hodder and Stoughton

NSPCC (undated) *Understanding the Links: Child abuse, animal abuse and domestic violence*, London: NSPCC

NHS (2012) *Pet Allergies and Pet Hygiene*, available at: www.nhs.uk/Livewell/Allergies/Pages/pet-hygiene.aspx

NHS Health and Social Care Information Centre (HSCIC) (2012) *Provisional Monthly Hospital Episode Statistics for Admitted Patient Care, Outpatients and Accident and Emergency Data*, London: NHS

NHS (2013a) *Toxoplasmosis*, available at: www.nhs.uk/conditions/Toxoplasmosis/Pages/Introduction.aspx

NHS (2013b) *Toxocariasis*, available at: www.nhs.uk/conditions/Toxocariasis/Pages/Introduction.aspx

NHS (2013c) *Preventing Toxocariasis*, available at: www.nhs.uk/Conditions/Toxocariasis/Pages/Prevention.aspx

O'Haire M (2010) 'Companion animals and human health: benefits, challenges and the road ahead', *Journal of Veterinary Behaviour*, 5:5, pp 226–234

PFMA (2014) *Pet Population 2013*, available at: www.pfma.org.uk/pet-population/

Public Health England (2011) *Reducing the Risks of Salmonella Infection from Reptiles*, available at: www.gov.uk/government/uploads/system/uploads/attachment_data/file/330580/Reducing_the_risks_of_salmonella_infection_from_reptiles.pdf

Public Health England (2012) *Control of Psittacosis*, available at: https://assets.publishing.service.gov.uk/government/uploads/system/uploads/attachment_data/file/563418/V_57i2.1.pdf

Public Health England (2014) *Background Information on Psittacosis*, available at: www.hpa.org.uk/Topics/InfectiousDiseases/InfectionsAZ/Psittacosis/GeneralInformation/psiBackgroundInformation/

Rockett B (2014) *Attachment Relationships in Long-Term Foster Care: The function and role of animals*, Bath: University of Bath, unpublished PhD thesis

Rockett B and Carr S (2014) 'Animals and attachment theory', *Society and Animals*, 22:4, pp 415–433

RSPCA (2012) *Growing up with a Dog*, London: RSPCA

RSPCA (undated) *FAQ: Can you feed live prey to a pet snake?*, available at: www.rspca.org.uk/utilities/contactus/reportcruelty

Stilwell V (2005) *It's Me or the Dog*, London: Harper Collins

Thomas C, Beckford V, Lowe N and Murch M (1999) *Adopted Children Speaking*, London: BAAF

Tuzeo-Jarolmen J (2007) *When a Family Pet Dies: A guide to dealing with children's loss*, London: Jessica Kingsley Publishers

Welfare in Dog Training (2010) *What's Wrong with using "Dominance" to Explain the Behaviour of Dogs?*, available at: www.dogwelfarecampaign.org/why-not-dominance.php

Westgarth C (2010) 'Dogs and children', *FosterTalk Magazine*, pp 10–11

Zilcha-Mano S, Mikulincer M and Shaver P (2011) 'Pet in the therapy room: an attachment perspective on animal-assisted therapy', *Attachment and Human Development*, 13:6, pp 541–561

Useful organisations

Association of Pet Behaviour Counsellors – www.apbc.org.uk

Association of Pet Dog Trainers – www.apdt.co.uk

Blue Cross – www.bluecross.org.uk

Blue Dog – www.thebluedog.org/en/

British Veterinary Association – www.bva.co.uk

Buttercups Sanctuary for Goats – www.buttercups.org.uk

Cats Protection – www.cats.org.uk

Dogs Trust – www.dogstrust.org.uk

People's Dispensary for Sick Animals (PDSA) – www.pdsa.org.uk

Pets as Therapy – www.petsastherapy.org

Royal College of Veterinary Surgeons – www.rcvs.org.uk

Royal Society for the Prevention of Cruelty to Animals (RSPCA) – www.rspca.org.uk

Safer Pets – www.saferpets.co.uk

The Kennel Club – www.thekennelclub.org.uk

Appendix A
CoramBAAF dog assessment form

A sample of this form is also available in the members' section of the CoramBAAF website. Both the dog assessment and pet assessment forms are provided free to all licence holders of CoramBAAF's fostering and adoption assessment forms.

This form (© CoramBAAF) is intended for completion by the assessing social worker in partnership with the applicant(s) or foster carer(s) who will hold much of the information. It does not assume that the assessing social worker to have any specialist knowledge of dogs, but they should be familiar with the CoramBAAF Good Practice Guide, *Dogs and Pets in Fostering and Adoption* (Adams, 2015). Completion of this assessment form should indicate whether advice should be sought from someone with an expertise in dog behaviour and psychology. One form should be used for each dog.

BASIC DETAILS

Name of owner(s)			
Name of dog			
Sex	Male/Female	Neutered?	Yes/No
Date of birth		Age	
Breed			
Breed information			

PERSONALITY AND HISTORY

Describe the dog's personality and general behaviour

Describe what is known about the dog's history

LIVING ARRANGEMENTS, TRAINING AND ROUTINES

Where does the dog live and sleep?

What are the dog's daily routines?

Has the dog been formally or informally trained?

To what extent will the dog follow basic commands?

HEALTH AND HYGIENE

What are the arrangements for feeding the dog?

Where does the dog toilet and, if applicable, how is the waste disposed of?

Does the dog have routine vaccinations and preventative treatment for worms, fleas and lice, etc?	
Is the dog registered with a vet?	Yes/No
Is the dog covered by health insurance or other arrangements?	Yes/No
If the answer is "no" to either of the above, then provide details below	
Details/any further information in relation to health and hygiene	

SAFETY

How does the dog respond to other dogs?
How does the dog respond to people in public and when they visit the home?
What contact does the dog have with children and how does s/he respond to them?

SAFETY CHECKLIST

Has the dog ever bitten anyone?	Yes/No
Has the dog ever snapped or snarled at anyone?	Yes/No
Has the dog ever shown signs of aggression to anyone?	Yes/No
Has the dog ever fought with another dog other than in play?	Yes/No
Does the dog chase and/or kill small animals?	Yes/No
Is the dog scared by crying babies/shouting children?	Yes/No
Does the dog get overly excited when people run around?	Yes/No
If the answer is "yes" to any of the above, then provide details below and give careful consideration as to whether a specialist dog assessment is required.	
Can the owner touch the dog's food bowl when eating?	Yes/No
Can the owner remove toys from the dog if very excited?	Yes/No
Does the dog tolerate being stroked/physically examined?	Yes/No
Can the owner push the dog around in a playful manner?	Yes/No
Has the dog been neutered?	Yes/No

If the answer is "no" to any of the above, then provide details below and give careful consideration as to whether a specialist dog assessment is required.

Is a specialist dog assessment necessary because of answers above or for any other reason?	Yes/No
Details/further information	

BREEDING/EMPLOYMENT

If the owners use their home for breeding, grooming or running kennels, then set out the implications of this for fostering or adoption (using an additional page).

SOCIAL WORKER'S OBSERVATIONS

Assessing social worker's observations of the dog during visits to the home, including any comments on behaviour, hygiene or safety

SOCIAL WORKER'S SUMMARY AND ANALYSIS

Suitability/significance of this dog in relation to fostering or adoption
What action, if any, needs to be taken to reduce any foreseeable risks?

Name of assessing social worker	
Signature of assessing social worker	
Agency	
Date	

APPLICANT'S/FOSTER CARER'S DECLARATION

- The information provided above is factually correct and I/we have shared fully and honestly all the relevant information regarding our dog.

- I/We have read and understand the information provided in Chapter 4 of the CoramBAAF Good Practice Guide, *Dogs and Pets in Fostering and Adoption* (Adams, 2015).

- I/We undertake to provide any necessary supervision of the dog and child or children to minimise risk of harm to either.

Any comments

Signature of applicant/foster carer 1	
Date	
Signature of applicant/foster carer 2	
Date	

Appendix B
CoramBAAF pet assessment form

A sample of this form is also available in the members' section of the CoramBAAF website. Both the dog assessment and pet assessment forms are provided free to all licence holders of CoramBAAF's fostering and adoption assessment forms.

This form (© CoramBAAF) is intended for completion by the assessing social worker in partnership with the applicant(s) or foster carer(s) who will hold much of the information. It does not assume that the assessing social worker to have any specialist knowledge of the pets, but they should be familiar with the CoramBAAF Good Practice Guide, *Dogs and Pets in Fostering and Adoption* (Adams, 2015).

BASIC DETAILS

Name of owner(s)	
Name of animal(s)	
Type of animal(s)	

DESCRIPTION

Describe the animal or animals, including any relevant information about their personality, history and how they were acquired.

HOUSING AND ROUTINES

> Describe where the animal or animals live within the home, including routines such as feeding and grooming.

HEALTH AND HYGIENE

Describe any issues in relation to health and hygiene, and how they will be managed.	
Does the animal have routine vaccinations and preventative treatment?	
Is the animal registered with a vet?	Yes/No
If the answer is "no", then provide details below.	

SAFETY

> Describe any safety issues and how they will be managed.

BREEDING/EMPLOYMENT

> If the owners use their home for breeding or any income-generating activity, then set out the implications of this for fostering or adoption (using an additional page).

SOCIAL WORKER'S OBSERVATIONS

> Assessing social worker's observations of the animal or animals during visits to the home, including any comments on behaviour, hygiene or safety

SOCIAL WORKER'S SUMMARY AND ANALYSIS

> Suitability/significance of the animal or animals in relation to fostering or adoption

> What action, if any, needs to be taken to reduce any foreseeable risks?

Name of assessing social worker	
Signature of assessing social worker	
Agency	
Date	

APPLICANT'S/FOSTER CARER'S DECLARATION

- The information provided above is factually correct and I/we have shared fully and honestly all the relevant information regarding our pet(s).

- I/We undertake to provide any necessary activity to minimise the risk of harm to child or children and pet(s).

Any comments

Signature of applicant/foster carer 1	
Date	
Signature of applicant/foster carer 2	
Date	

Appendix C
CoramBAAF dog assessment form (example)

This form (© CoramBAAF) is intended for completion by the assessing social worker in partnership with the applicant(s) or foster carer(s) who will hold much of the information. It does not assume that the assessing social worker to have any specialist knowledge of dogs, but they should be familiar with the CoramBAAF Good Practice Guide, *Dogs and Pets in Fostering and Adoption* (Adams, 2014). Completion of this assessment form should indicate whether advice should be sought from someone with an expertise in dog behaviour and psychology. One form should be used for each dog.

BASIC DETAILS

Name of owner(s)	Sarah and Paul		
Name of dog	Bluebell (Bluey)		
Sex	Female	Neutered?	Yes
Date of birth	June 2010 (estimate)	Age	3 years
Breed	German Wirehaired Pointer		
Breed information	The Kennel Club Breed Information Centre notes that the German Wirehaired Pointer was originally a gun dog and describes the breed as 'easily trained and friendly, he has a tough, cheerful appearance, making him good as a family dog as he is a worker'.		

PERSONALITY AND HISTORY

Describe the dog's personality and general behaviour

The applicants write:

Bluey is blind and we understand that she has been blind from birth, and although this seems to have minimal impact on her practical day-to-day functioning, it does potentially impact on her emotional well-being. She wants to know what is happening around her, and since she can't see, will feel with her nose, which can be annoying if you are trying to do something and you keep getting nudged! At times this can be experienced as her being bossy.

We feel that Bluey is a lovely natured dog who is generally content with life. She enjoys one or two walks each day (including runs in the forest most days) and is happy sleeping at our feet while one of us is working at our desk. In the evenings she settles really easily after dinner. She sleeps well and does not disturb us, even if we have a lie in. We do leave her with close friends and relatives for a few days at a time and she manages this easily. People are surprised how easily she finds her bearings in new environments.

In some ways she can be dominant – she pushes Simba (our other dog) to get herself comfortable in the car – but gives no indication of trying to dominate people. She can be jealous of Simba and if he is getting attention such as grooming she will push her way forward to make sure she doesn't miss out. This may be in part about her blindness and not being sure exactly what is happening. She does not have the same issue with humans.

Describe what is known about the dog's history

The applicants write:

We got Bluey from a rescue centre one year ago. She was estimated to be about two years old at this time and we know she was originally rescued from Ireland and has had at least three homes before she came to us.

She came to us from a family home with two children, where those children were very attached to her and she was said to be very good with them. This family said that they could not keep Bluey (having had her for a month) because they had other elderly dogs and did not have the time to exercise them all (saying they needed different levels of exercise), and because their home was really too small for a blind dog. They were clearly upset about having to rehome her but felt she would make a lovely family pet in the right setting.

Our guess (and it is only that) is that she has not been physically harmed by people in the past as she shows no fear or nervousness around people, but we do wonder if she has been left to fend for herself as she will eat anything left unattended (including from worktops).

LIVING ARRANGEMENTS, TRAINING AND ROUTINES

Where does the dog live and sleep?
Bluey has a bed under the stairs that she shares with Simba, but sometimes one of them will sleep on another dog bed by the fire. Bluey has access to all downstairs parts of the house and the upstairs office, but will not go up the stairs that lead to the bedrooms (a different staircase).

What are the dog's daily routines?
Bluey is said to fit easily into different daily routines, according to what the applicants are doing that day. She eats in the morning and evening, and will get one or two walks each day, at least one of these in the local forest. She is very happy sleeping when Sarah or Paul are working in the office. If the routine needs to change at short notice, Bluey adapts easily to this, and can be left at home for periods up to four hours. Sarah and Paul anticipate walking the dogs when the children are at school, or one of them will do it, or they will include children in dog walking, depending on the specific circumstances.

Has the dog been formally or informally trained?
Bluey went to formal dog training classes for about three months when she first joined Sarah and Paul but they report that she made limited progress. They have undertaken some training of her but her ability to learn is limited (see below).

To what extent will the dog follow basic commands?
The applicants write: *Bluey has always been house-trained but it appears that she had very little other training before coming to us. Since then she has been trained to sit nicely for snacks or dinner and will sit with a treat on the floor next to her until given permission to eat it. Her recall is usually good, but not entirely reliable.* *Bluey's walking on a lead – although much improved – still requires work, and we have noticed that she does worst on country walks with the accompanying smells of wildlife. It is difficult to train Bluey because she tends to get overexcited at the idea of food rewards, making her unable to focus on what is being asked of her.* *When we first got Bluey, she had a tendency to jump up with her front paws and we have worked very hard to address this. For the most part this behaviour has ceased, but it can re-emerge when she is very excited (e.g. when one of us returns from being away) and we continue to work on this. We are also very careful to manage this with visitors.*

HEALTH AND HYGIENE

What are the arrangements for feeding the dog?	
Bluey is fed raw meat, either purchased as dog mince or "flank" from the local butcher that Sarah and Paul cut up and freeze into suitably sized packs. She eats this from her dog bowl in the kitchen, and occasionally she will get a meaty bone and will eat this outside in the garden.	
Where does the dog toilet and, if applicable, how is the waste disposed of?	
Bluey will toilet either on forest walks, or in a part of the garden closest to the house. This is collected by Sarah and Paul on a regular basis and disposed of in an area of overgrown vegetation that is not accessible to household members (on their property but over the perimeter fence).	
Does the dog have routine vaccinations and preventative treatment for worms, fleas and lice, etc?	
Bluey has been vaccinated as advised by the vet and attends for annual boosters. Sarah and Paul use recommended three-monthly treatments for worms, fleas and lice.	
Is the dog registered with a vet?	Yes
Is the dog covered by health insurance or other arrangements?	No
If the answer is "no" to either of the above then provide details below	
Details/any further information in relation to health and hygiene?	
Owners will use savings to cover significant veterinary costs.	

SAFETY

How does the dog respond to other dogs?
The applicants write:
We have had no reason to think that Bluey is aggressive with other dogs. She gets on very well with our other dog Simba (and, we are told, historically with other dogs) and has been fine with other dogs at training class and when we have met them during walks. We are, however, mindful of her being blind, and the dog trainer suggested being careful about meeting other dogs as she might feel vulnerable. She can lurch towards other dogs if they approach her face when she is on the lead, but has never snapped or appeared to be "going for them". When she is off the lead, or once she knows the other dog, she is more relaxed.
How does the dog respond to people in public and when they visit the home?
The applicants write:
Bluey is very relaxed with people in public and is always happy to be stroked, or to sit and wait. She will bark at people who come to the home but we believe this is about her not knowing who they are, and she quickly stops once they have entered, or with reassurance.
When we have had friends and their children visiting, Bluey quickly settles into accepting them as part of the household and there is no sense of her being jealous if she is not getting attention. She happily gets on with her own routines, taking the opportunity for some extra petting where available.
What contact does the dog have with children and how does s/he respond to them?
The applicants write:
When children have visited our home (sometimes for a few days at a time; sometimes for a few hours), Bluey has adapted well. She tends to be happy having them around, and really enjoys being stroked and groomed. Other than that, she tends to happily coexist rather than interact meaningfully – primarily because her play is limited.
Whereas children will get lots of fun out of Simba, Bluey is not really a playful dog and prefers to wander about sniffing in hedges and running up and down. We are also mindful that she might run into children when outside and friend's children have quickly learned – like us – to let her know where they are by making appropriate noises!
There was one occasion when a 10-year-old was trying to teach her tricks and in her excitement to get the reward she raised her paw and scratched his face. He was kneeling on the ground at her head height when this happened, and we have learned from this and would supervise such activity more carefully.

SAFETY CHECKLIST

Has the dog ever bitten anyone?	No
Has the dog ever snapped or snarled at anyone?	No
Has the dog ever shown signs of aggression to anyone?	No
Has the dog ever fought with another dog other than in play?	No
Does the dog chase and/or kill small animals?	No
Is the dog scared by crying babies/shouting children?	No
Does the dog get overly excited when people run around?	No (see below)
If the answer is "yes" to any of the above, then provide details below and give careful consideration as to whether a specialist dog assessment is required	
Can the owner touch the dog's food bowl when eating?	Yes
Can the owner remove toys from the dog if very excited?	Yes
Does the dog tolerate being stroked/physically examined?	Yes
Can the owner push the dog around in a playful manner?	Yes
Has the dog been neutered?	Yes
If the answer is "no" to any of the above, then provide details below and give careful consideration as to whether a specialist dog assessment is required	
Is a specialist dog assessment necessary because of answers above or for any other reason?	No
Details/further information	
There is no indication that Bluey is an aggressive dog, although she can present a risk of knocking a small child over. When Simba is running around, Bluey might bark and try to join in, but is limited by her blindness. The prospective adopters are specifically looking at older children, and have a good understanding of how to manage Bluey in this context.	

BREEDING/EMPLOYMENT

If the owners use their home for breeding, grooming or running kennels, then set out the implications of this for adoption or fostering (using an additional page)

SOCIAL WORKER'S OBSERVATIONS

Assessing social worker's observations of the dog during visits to the home, including any comments on behaviour, hygiene or safety
I have visited regularly and have never had any concerns about Bluey. She has been interested in sniffing me on arrival but settled down quickly, sometimes after encouragement from her owners, and slept during most of the time we were talking. There have never been any hygiene concerns regarding the dog. I also spoke to one of the referees who confirmed that he had visited with his toddler and stayed for a week. Bluey was encouraged to stay away from the child and she managed this without difficulty.

SOCIAL WORKER'S SUMMARY AND ANALYSIS

Suitability/significance of this dog in relation to adoption or fostering
While Bluey does present some risk of bumping into a child inadvertently, this risk is mitigated by the age of the children being considered for adoption, and the fact that the likely consequences are no more than usual childhood bumps and bruises. The applicants have managed children staying in their home for extended periods without any problems, and are very mindful of potential risks. In all other respects there are no identified issues, and no reason to think that Bluey is problematic in relation to the adoption application.

Bluey is clearly a full canine member of this family, and children will be expected to treat her kindly and respectfully. |
| What action, if any, needs to be taken to reduce any foreseeable risks? |
| None. |

Name of assessing social worker	Social worker
Signature of assessing social worker	Social worker
Date	1 June 2013

APPLICANT'S/ FOSTER CARER'S DECLARATION

- The information provided above is factually correct and I/we have shared fully and honestly all the relevant information regarding our dog.

- I/We have read and understand the information provided in Chapter 4 of the CoramBAAF Good Practice Guide, *Dogs and Pets in Fostering and Adoption* (Adams, 2015).

- I/We undertake to provide any necessary supervision of the dog and child or children to minimise risk of harm to either.

Any comments:
We know that Bluey does present some challenges, but feel that we have a good understanding of her nature and likely behaviour, and feel that she is very manageable with children in the household, particularly as we are not interested in adopting babies or toddlers.
We do accept that there is always the risk that Bluey might accidently knock over a child if she bumps into them when they are not looking, but against that we actually think that she can be a great help in teaching children about being responsible and helping to care for others who need that.

Signature of applicant/foster carer 1	Sarah
Date	4 June 2013
Signature of applicant/foster carer 2	Paul
Date	4 June 2013

Appendix D
CoramBAAF pet assessment form (example)

This form (© CoramBAAF) is intended for completion by the assessing social worker in partnership with the applicant(s) or foster carer(s) who will hold much of the information. It does not assume that the assessing social worker to have any specialist knowledge of the pets, but they should be familiar with the CoramBAAF Good Practice Guide, *Dogs and Pets in Fostering and Adoption* (Adams, 2015).

BASIC DETAILS

Name of owner(s)	Rose and Phil
Name of animal(s)	Nelson and Smudge
Type of animal(s)	Cats

DESCRIPTION

Describe the animal or animals including any relevant information about their personality, history and how they were acquired
Nelson and Smudge joined the family as kittens, being acquired from a friend in summer 2007. They are both now seven years old. Nelson is described as the shyer of the two with people he doesn't know, but once familiar with a person, enjoys being stroked and groomed. He sleeps a lot but enjoys going out hunting for birds and mice. Smudge is very affectionate and friendly. He is also a bit of a hunter, bringing home birds and small mammals (usually alive). Both enjoy playing with their cat toys and enjoy human involvement in this.

HOUSING AND ROUTINES

Describe where the animal or animals live within the home, including routines such as feeding and grooming.
The cats are allowed all over the house with the exception of the kitchen and what is currently the spare bedroom. The cats do sleep on Rose and Phil's bed, but will not be allowed to sleep on foster children's beds or go into their bedrooms.
The cats have dry food permanently available in the utility room, and fresh water that is changed daily. Sometimes they are given tinned cat food to supplement this. They are brushed every few days and appear well cared for.

HEALTH AND HYGIENE

Describe any issues in relation to health and hygiene, and how they will be managed.	
The cats will toilet outside and away from the garden. They have their own food utensils that are washed in a separate sink in the utility room, and stored separately from the household cutlery.	
Both cats do bring home dead or living birds and small mammals on a fairly regular basis. Rose and Phil respond by either releasing the animal (if alive) or disposing of it in the outside rubbish bin (if dead), and cleaning the floor as appropriate.	
Does the animal have routine vaccinations and preventative treatment?	
Both cats are wormed and treated for fleas, etc, as recommended by the vet. The treatments are kept in a high cupboard in the utility room.	
Is the animal registered with a vet?	Yes
If the answer is "no", then provide details below	

SAFETY

Describe any safety issues and how they will be managed.
Rose and Phil are mindful that cats can scratch and will encourage any foster children to approach them carefully and under supervision initially. Smudge is always happy to play with or be stroked by visiting children, but Nelson is more likely to remove himself when new people visit the home.

BREEDING/EMPLOYMENT

If the owners use their home for breeding or any income generating activity, then set out the implications of this for adoption fostering (using an additional page).

SOCIAL WORKER'S OBSERVATIONS

Assessing social worker's observations of the animal or animals during visits to the home, including any comments on behaviour, hygiene or safety.
The cats have been around during most of my visits and Smudge has been happy for me to stroke him. I have also stroked Nelson when he was asleep on the chair. He rolled over to have his tummy tickled and then went back to sleep.

SOCIAL WORKER'S SUMMARY AND ANALYSIS

Suitability/significance of animal or animals in relation to fostering
The cats appear friendly and are used to children visiting. They are well cared for and there are no concerns regarding hygiene. Phil and Rose are mindful of the need to manage children's interactions with the cats, but feel confident that if they were scared or uncomfortable the cats would seek to run away rather than retaliate. There is no reason to think that these pets are not compatible with fostering.
What action, if any, needs to be taken to reduce any foreseeable risks?
None.

Name of assessing social worker	Social worker
Signature of assessing social worker	Social worker
Date	3 July 2014

APPLICANT'S/FOSTER CARER'S DECLARATION

- The information provided above is factually correct and I/we have shared fully and honestly all the relevant information regarding our pet(s).

- I/We undertake to provide any necessary activity to minimise the risk of harm to child or children and pet(s).

Any comments:
We agree with what is written above.

Signature of applicant/foster carer 1	Phil
Date	3 July 2014
Signature of applicant/foster carer 2	Rose
Date	3 July 2014